I0829613

Stop My OCD

A Practitioner's Guide to Treating OCD and Incorporating Virtual Reality.

Andrew E. Colsky
JD, LLM, LPC, LMHC

© 2024 Copyright by Andrew E. Colsky, JD, LLM, LPC, LMHC
Stop My OCD

All Rights Reserved.

No part of this publication may be reproduced, distributed, or transmitted in any form or by any means, including photocopying, recording, or other electronic or mechanical methods, without the prior written permission of the author and publisher, except in the case of brief quotations embedded in reviews and certain other noncommercial uses permitted by copyright law.

Dedication

I dedicate this book to all of the Obsessive Compulsive Disorder (OCD) researchers who have worked tirelessly to understand and develop treatments for OCD. Without their work, I would not have been able to do my work. I also dedicate this book to individuals living with OCD and their loved ones and caregivers. Obsessive doubt and intrusive thoughts can cause a lot of distress for many people in different ways. By educating ourselves and responding with compassion, we can all find effective ways to address OCD.

Contents

Chapter One
Obsessive Compulsive Disorder

What is Obsessive-Compulsive Disorder (OCD)

Obsessive-compulsive disorder (OCD) is characterized by the presence of obsessions and/or compulsions. Obsessions are intrusive thoughts, urges, or images that are recurrent, persistent, and unwanted. Obsessions cause marked distress or anxiety, leading to attempts to ignore, suppress, or neutralize them with another thought or action. Compulsions are repetitive behaviors (e.g., handwashing and checking) or mental acts (e.g., praying, counting, or silently repeating words/phrases) that an individual feels compelled to perform in response to an obsession or in accordance with a set of rigid rules. Compulsions are intended to reduce distress or to prevent some type of harm or disaster, are excessive, and may be completely unrelated to the content of the obsessions.

To meet the criteria for OCD, the DSM-V (APA, 2013) requires the following: (A) the presence of obsessions, compulsions, or both; (B) the obsessions or compulsions are time-consuming (e.g., take more than one hour per day) or cause clinically significant distress or impairment in social, occupational, or other important areas of functioning; and the distress and symptoms are not better explained by another mental disorder. Clinicians should specify *with good or fair insight* when the individual recognizes that the OCD beliefs are false, probably not true, or that they may not be true. The specifier *with poor insight* should be used when the individual thinks OCD beliefs are probably true, while the specifier *with absent insight/delusional beliefs* describes individuals who are completely convinced that OCD beliefs are true.

Causes of OCD

OCD is a complex neuropsychological disorder. Research has shown that there is a significant genetic component to OCD. Twin and family studies have yielded heritability estimates of around 50%, while a large study of individuals from the Swedish National Patient Register produced a heritability estimate of 35% after accounting for maternal effects and assortative mating (Fernandez et al., 2018; Mahjani et al., 2020; Mataix-Cols et al., 2013). While these studies indicate that there is a sizable genetic component to OCD, specific genes related to OCD have not been identified. Most mental health practitioners believe that OCD symptoms occur when interactions between genetic and environmental factors cause dysfunction within networks of connected brain regions.

Based on studies using functional brain imaging, neuropsychologists concluded that OCD symptoms result from hyperactivity in several brain regions, including the orbitofrontal cortex, the anterior cingulate cortex, portions of the basal ganglia (especially the caudate nucleus), and the thalamus (Goodman et al., 2021). The orbital frontal cortex is the brain region responsible for detecting when something is awry and works with other brain structures (like the anterior cingulate cortex) to address the issue and form a plan to manage the situation.

In OCD, the orbital frontal cortex may perceive that the doorknob is germy and dangerous and then send this warning signal to the thalamus. The thalamus receives sensory information from various parts of the brain and further processes the information before sending it to the brain regions associated with planning, decision-making, and action. In people without OCD, the caudate nucleus functions as a brake that prevents unfounded worries from consuming brain resources. This brake malfunctions in people with OCD and does not suppress these warning signals from the orbital frontal cortex, causing the thalamus to be overloaded with warning signals. Because the brake for this circuit is malfunctioning, a situation that could be resolved with ordinary handwashing now triggers a contamination obsession that results in excessive, ritualized washing.

As OCD progresses, the circuits underlying this cycle are strengthened, meaning that obsessions and compulsions may be triggered by a wide range of stimuli or even in the absence of any triggering stimuli. It is important to note that activity levels within these brain regions normalize with effective treatment for OCD, whether treatment involves SSRIs, psychotherapy using exposure and response prevention, or both (Goodman et al., 2021).

Disruptions in neurotransmitter systems also play a role in OCD symptomatology. People with OCD often experience decreases in symptoms when treated with selective serotonin reuptake inhibitors (SSRIs), which suggests that dysfunction in the brain's serotonergic system is involved in OCD. Additionally, animal studies have shown that medications that alter glutamate levels cause excessive grooming behaviors, leading researchers to speculate that the neurotransmitter glutamate may also play a role in OCD (Goodman et al., 2021).

Important Concepts in OCD

Ego-syntonic vs Ego-dystonic

To better understand OCD, it is helpful to understand the definitions of ego-syntonic and ego-dystonic. These words are used in psychology to describe the relationship between an individual's thoughts or behaviors and their sense of self or identity. These terms are often used in the context of mental disorders, particularly in the field of psychopathology.

1. Ego-syntonic:

Ego-syntonic refers to thoughts, beliefs, or behaviors that are consistent with an individual's self-perception and are in harmony with their overall sense of identity. These thoughts or behaviors are generally comfortable and acceptable to the person experiencing them. They do not cause significant distress or conflict with their self-image. People with ego-syntonic thoughts may be unaware or less motivated to change their behavior because it aligns with their core beliefs. Ego-syntonic thoughts and behaviors are generally associated with obsessive-compulsive personality disorder (OCPD).

Example: An individual with OCPD who feels a strong need to maintain symmetry and cleanliness views these actions as ego-syntonic. They perceive these rituals as necessary for maintaining order and preventing harm, and they do not experience distress from engaging in them.

2. Ego-dystonic:

In contrast, ego-dystonic describes thoughts, beliefs, or behaviors that are inconsistent with an individual's self-perception or sense of identity. These thoughts and behaviors typically cause distress, discomfort, or conflict because they go against the person's values, desires, or ideals. Individuals with ego-dystonic thoughts and behaviors often recognize the inconsistency and may experience a strong motivation to change or alleviate these thoughts. Ego-dystonic thoughts and behaviors are hallmarks of OCD.

Example: A person experiencing intrusive thoughts of harming others but having no desire to act on them finds these thoughts to be ego-dystonic. The thoughts are inconsistent with their moral compass and cause significant distress, as they go against their core values and desires.

In summary, ego-syntonic thoughts and behaviors align with an individual's sense of self and do not cause significant distress, while ego-dystonic thoughts and behaviors are inconsistent with an individual's self-perception and often result in distress or conflict. Understanding the distinction between these two concepts can be crucial in diagnosing and treating certain mental disorders.

The OCD Cycle

People who have OCD find themselves trapped in a cycle of obsessions and compulsions. Obsessions are highly distressing and ego-dystonic, meaning that they are not consistent with the person's goals and values, like having intrusive thoughts of harming loved ones. However, since many obsessions involve things that are highly important to people, like safety, cleanliness, well-being, relationships, identity, and religious faith/spiritual traditions, the intrusive thoughts and images cause considerable distress, leading to high levels of anxiety, fear, and/or disgust. People with OCD perform compulsions, or rituals, to reduce distress or counteract the obsession, but the compulsions only provide temporary relief.

Without treatment, the cycle of obsessions and compulsions tends to increase in frequency and severity. The temporary decrease in distress following the performance of the compulsion reinforces the compulsion, strengthening the connection between obsessions and compulsions. Additionally, performing the compulsion prevents the individual from testing the OCD belief related to the obsession, which strengthens the individual's belief that performing the compulsion prevented the feared event from happening.

For example, a person with OCD may walk out of an important meeting after having the intrusive thought, "What if I forgot to put my parking brake on and my car rolls down the hill and kills a child?" The distress caused by this intrusive thought compels the individual to go check her car. Checking, and seeing that her parking brake was engaged, brings a sense of relief, and reduces her distress, which reinforces the checking behavior, making it more likely that she will engage in checking behavior the next time she has an intrusive thought. When she has a similar intrusive thought later in the day, she is likely to engage in checking behavior, having attributed the earlier aversion of disaster to checking her brake. She may think, "Well, last time my brake was on, but what if this time it's not?"

The primary language patients with OCD use in response to challenges to their obsessions is "yeah, but what if…" or "If I could just know for sure …" Seeking absolute certainty is a core component of OCD and one of the reasons why talk therapy is not effective for these patients. Certainty is the carrot that OCD continually dangles in front of people, telling them that if they would only clean something just right, or say the perfect prayer, or any number of other compulsions, they can be certain of averting disaster. As unreasonable or unlikely as obsessions may be, absolute certainty of what the future holds is not possible. There is a chance that you could get sick from touching a doorknob and sometimes devastating things happen. Effective therapy for OCD involves helping patients recognize and accept that uncertainty is real, unavoidable, and tolerable.

The obsessions involved in OCD cause such significant distress that individuals are extremely resistant to testing them. The individual may think that it is better to perform a quick compulsion or ritual than to risk the harm the obsession suggests. However, this intolerance of uncertainty and inability to manage distress further strengthens the OCD cycle and leads to increasingly time-consuming and elaborate compulsions. For many individuals with OCD, symptoms will continue to increase in frequency and intensity, causing significant impairments in functioning.

In their inference-based conceptualization of OCD, O'Connor and Aardema discuss "pathological doubt" and explain that people with OCD often disregard sensory information from the current reality, and focus on the obsession instead (Julien, O'Conner, & Aardema, 2016). With my patients, I refer to this tendency as "obsessive doubt" and use the OCD cycle to clarify how disregarding their current sensory reality gets them stuck in an endless cycle of obsessions and compulsions. Refer to the following graphic for a breakdown of what happens in OCD.

OCD Cycle Graphic

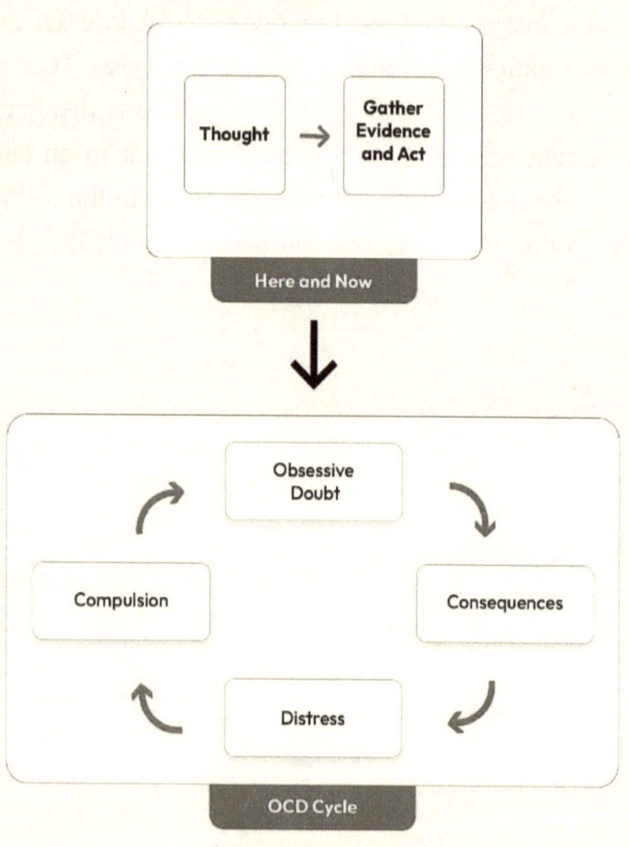

You can be enjoying your day without a worry in the world and suddenly have a thought. There may or may not be an overt trigger as to why you had this thought, but a trigger exists, nonetheless. Let's take the thought "My hands may be dirty." Okay, your hands may indeed be dirty. You then seek evidence to validate or invalidate your thought. You use facts and your senses to do this. Your senses tell you what you see, smell, taste, touch, hear. You also have the benefit of facts, meaning that you know where your hands have been. For example, you could have just changed a tire on your car. In that case, you know that you have been touching a dirty tire. You can also see grease and dirt on your hands and feel grit and grime. They probably smell bad as well. As a result, you wash your hands and move on with your day. All of this happened in the "here and now" box in the graphic. Notice how everything in that box is ego-syntonic and you never entered the OCD cycle.

Now let's consider another example. Again, you have the thought that your hands may be dirty. As a result, you seek clarification. But this time, you know that you just returned from the restroom 10 minutes ago where you washed your hands with soap and water before leaving. You did not touch anything dirty and when you look at your hands, you neither see any dirt nor do you feel anything on them. There is no evidence that your hands are dirty. At this point, most people just move on with whatever they were doing. However, a person with OCD does not have that same experience.

If you have OCD, you will cross the divide from the ego-syntonic "here and now" and enter the ego-dystonic OCD cycle. First, you find yourself in the obsessive doubt phase. Obsessive doubt is when you have the evidence to confirm or disconfirm your thought, but you just don't believe it. Obsessive doubt has its very own lexicon which will be described below. In the obsessive doubt phase of the OCD cycle, your OCD tries to use doubt in terms of "what-if" thinking to challenge the facts you have with unsubstantiated and unprovable possibilities. "What if my hands are really dirty and I just didn't see it?"

Once you enter the OCD cycle, you will go through all four phases, from obsessive doubt to consequences, to distress, and finally, to compulsion. There is no stopping it, at least without treatment. Obsessive doubt leads to thoughts of consequences and OCD loves the negative, even doomsday scenarios. "Well, if my hands are dirty, I could spread the contamination and get sick or even die!" Wow, that can certainly be scary! So, guess what happens? We feel distressed and distress makes us uncomfortable at the very least and can accelerate all the way to having a panic attack. At this point, all we want to do is to make it stop!

But we don't know what to do to eliminate our distress. This is where compulsions come in. A compulsion is something that we do to help reduce our distress. The upside is that it usually works and provides some relief. The downside is that the relief is always short-lived and eventually we cycle back to the obsessive doubt and start the OCD cycle all over again.

OCD Doubt Lexicon

OCD doubt has a language all its own that is designed to facilitate doubt. Obsessive doubt lexicon does not contain factual information. In my practice, I have identified the following elements in the OCD lexicon:

1. Things beyond your control

Things beyond our control are often attributed to "they," or their cousin "everybody." *"'They' must be thinking bad things about me."* As much as we may not like it, none of us controls what other people think. We also don't know what others are thinking. Even if we ask them, we have no way of knowing if they are telling us the truth. And my favorite question is "Who are *they*?" "They" seem to know a lot of things and do a lot of things. *"They say it's going to rain." "They are causing gas prices to skyrocket." "They are thinking that I made a fool of myself during my presentation."* And even if we were able to specifically identify who "they" are, there is nothing we can do about it. "They" also have a cousin: "Everybody." *"Everybody"* acts the same way as "They" do. But it can be even more devastating when *"Everybody" is thinking that I made a fool of myself.*

2. Emotion over logic

"Snakes scare me, so all snakes are bad." Sure, lots of people are afraid of snakes. I could write another book as to why this is the case but suffice it to say that this is a legitimate fear. However, a fear of snakes does not mean that all snakes are bad. In fact, snakes are generally more scared of us than we are of them. They just want to be left alone. If a snake bites, it is out of defense of itself or for food. The infamous rattle for which the rattlesnake is named serves as a warning to "go away and leave me alone and I will leave you alone." Snakes keep our insect and rodent populations in check which, in turn, cuts down on diseases spread by their prey. Logically, snakes don't want anything to do with us and they provide a lot of benefits.

3. Confirmation bias

Confirmation bias is the tendency to interpret any new evidence as supporting the belief we already held. Confirmation bias is literally everywhere we turn. People who spend a lot of time on the internet or social media are inundated with information that supports their own beliefs. People select specific news media because it presents information congruent with their own worldview.

A very common compulsion is to conduct research on the content of obsessive doubt. If my OCD says that fertilizer can be a harmful chemical, I can research the dangers of fertilizer and find unlimited information to substantiate my suspicion. But how much time did I spend researching the benefits or safety of fertilizer? When in the OCD cycle, the answer is probably none. This issue is even more pronounced when you read about #6, "overgeneralization."

4. Complex over simple thinking

Ockham's razor, a philosophical principle attributed to the medieval philosopher William Ockham, states that "The simplest explanation is usually the best one." OCD tends to disagree. Consider an individual who knows he has been touching a lot of things in a crowded public space. He is unable to wash his hands and would like to eat something. He may opt to use a fork and knife to eat his food so that he does not touch it with his hands, thus feeling safe. Someone with OCD may see this scenario very differently. She may think, my hands could be dirty and contaminated with all sorts of germs. I want to wash them but there is nowhere to do so. I could use a fork and knife to eat my food but if I do that, the germs could crawl off my hands, down the fork, and get all over my food. Therefore, it is only safe if I do not eat at all. Of course, the same logic could apply to the statement that "my feet are on the ground so germs could crawl up my leg to my arm and down to my fork and food. Thus, there is never any escape from germs.

5. Possibility becomes probability

This concept is an OCD favorite and makes any concept unclear. People with OCD seek clarity. Thus, the perfect trap is laid with this one thought. Every time you think you have a clear understanding of something, OCD chimes in with "it could" or "it's possible" or another form of the same thought.

Consider that millions of people are driving cars at any given moment. Some of them get into accidents. The data shows that it is a very small percentage, but it does indeed happen. It is true that if you drive a car, there is a *possibility* that you could get into an accident. But every single driver takes that risk whenever they drive. Someone with OCD modifies the reality that it is *possible* that they could get into an accident and turns it into the belief that if they drive, it is *probable* that they will get into an accident. OCD does this despite clear evidence against this belief.

6. Overgeneralization

In the OCD cycle, information is distorted to fit expectations. If I fear chlorine, I can find data showing it is harmful. But I conveniently ignore how much chlorine was studied, in what concentration, and how it was used. We swim in it and use it to make our drinking water safe, yet I choose to ignore these facts or overgeneralize and decide that swimming and tap water will harm me, even though they don't harm anybody else. Another favorite is bleach. The word "bleach" applies to many different actual chemicals. We can bleach our clothes, teeth, and hair, yet in overgeneralization, if we see the word "bleach," we assume it is a harmful form.

Bleaches come in many forms, all very different from each other and designed for specific purposes. There are:

chlorine bleach (sodium hypochlorite), oxygen bleach (hydrogen peroxide) used to clean wounds, non-chlorine bleach, which is a bleach alternative, color-safe bleach, natural bleaches, and more. In OCD overgeneralization, these are all the same in the patient's mind and they are all harmful; even the ones designed to sanitize our wounds!

7. Anecdotes

Anecdotes are short stories about real-life incidents. OCD frequently uses anecdotes in confirmation bias. OCD takes an anecdote and supplements it with unproven assumptions to reach an unrealistic conclusion. One could have had a real experience as a child where a dog bit their hand. OCD takes that anecdote and adds in unproven assumptions to create the thought "When I was a child, a dog bit my hand, which means that this dog that just walked into the room is probably going to bite me." OCD completely disregards that in the current situation, the dog is on a leash, wagging its tail, and rolling on the ground with its belly up in a submissive state.

8. Hearsay

Hearsay is information provided by another person that cannot be substantiated because it is not first-hand. Many people have played the child's game called "telephone" where a group of children sit in a circle and one person starts with a statement that they whisper to the person next to them. This continues around the circle until the last person reports the message they received. The final message is assured to be different from the original message. For example, "I like dogs" may end up as "I slipped on a log." Consider the statement "I heard that Sam is afraid of horror movies." That is hearsay. We do not know for sure whether Sam is afraid of horror movies as the information did not come from Sam himself. Yet, in OCD, hearsay is readily accepted if it supports an obsessive doubt.

9. False causation (also known as magical thinking)

An individual with OCD may have a belief that others would consider to be unbelievable. For example, an individual may say "I avoid stepping on cracks to keep my mom from breaking her back." The speaker is sure of this belief because they have been doing these things without fail for ten years and during that whole time, their mother has not broken her back. That is an example of correlation, not causation. Stepping on cracks does not cause someone to break their back. It is also a correlation that in the last ten years, I did not step on a crack, and I aged ten years. Would you say that avoiding stepping on cracks caused you to age ten years? It is a correlation, not a cause.

Common OCD Types (common obsessions and compulsions)

The content of obsessions and compulsions associated with OCD can vary widely and individuals with this disorder often have highly specific, individualized OCD beliefs and rituals. However, there are certain themes that emerge consistently across OCD and most individuals' obsessions can be categorized into one (or more) of the following common types: contamination, false memory, harm, hit and run, intrusive thoughts, just right, magical thinking, perfectionism, pure obsessional, relationship, scrupulosity/religiosity, sexual orientation, and somatic.

Common Compulsions

For each of these categories of obsessions, there are associated compulsions, like elaborate cleaning rituals to manage distress caused by contamination obsessions or excessive body scanning related to somatic obsessions. These themes have been observed across cultures and may be associated with different underlying neural pathways.

Contamination

Contamination OCD, also known as contamination-related obsessive-compulsive disorder, is a subtype of OCD characterized by persistent and intrusive thoughts, fears, and concerns about contamination. Individuals with contamination OCD experience extreme anxiety and distress regarding the presence of dirt, germs, chemicals, or other substances they perceive as dirty or harmful. This leads them to engage in repetitive behaviors or rituals, such as excessive handwashing, avoiding certain places or objects, or seeking reassurance, to neutralize or alleviate their anxiety.

Contamination OCD can significantly impact daily functioning and quality of life, as individuals may spend large amounts of time and energy managing their obsessions and compulsions. In extreme cases, individuals with contamination OCD may be unable to leave their homes or interact with others due to contamination fears. They may constantly clean and disinfect their living spaces, including frequently washing their clothes or belongings. Additionally, they might have a strict set of rules or rituals for handling and preparing food to prevent contamination. These behaviors and rituals provide temporary relief from anxiety but can significantly disrupt daily life and cause distress.

False Memory

False memory OCD, also known as memory-related obsessive-compulsive disorder, is a subtype of OCD characterized by intrusive and distressing thoughts or doubts about past events, often involving harmful or socially unacceptable actions. Individuals with false memory OCD experience intense anxiety and uncertainty about the accuracy or truthfulness of their memories. They may have intrusive thoughts or doubts about committing acts they find morally repugnant, even if there is no evidence to support these thoughts. These intrusive thoughts can lead to a heightened sense of guilt, shame, and self-doubt.

Examples of false memory OCD might include obsessions about causing harm to someone, committing a crime, or engaging in inappropriate behavior, despite having no actual recollection or evidence of such events. Individuals with false memory OCD may engage in compulsive behaviors, such as repeatedly reviewing past events, seeking reassurance from others, or researching to find evidence that disproves their intrusive thoughts. Despite the absence of any real memories or evidence, false memory OCD can cause significant distress and interfere with daily functioning. It is important to note that false memory OCD does not involve intentionally creating false memories, but rather the anxiety and doubt associated with the fear of having a memory that is not supported by evidence.

Harm

Harm OCD, also known as harm-related obsessive-compulsive disorder, is a subtype of OCD characterized by intrusive and distressing thoughts, fears, or obsessions related to causing harm to oneself or others. Individuals with harm OCD experience intense anxiety, guilt, and fear associated with the possibility of acting on these intrusive thoughts, despite having no actual desire or intention to harm anyone. These obsessions are ego-dystonic, meaning they are inconsistent with an individual's core values and intentions.

Examples of harm OCD might include intrusive thoughts of physically assaulting a loved one, fears of being responsible for accidents or causing harm through negligence or worries about being a threat to others. Individuals with harm OCD may engage in various compulsive behaviors or rituals to prevent the feared harm, such as avoidance, seeking reassurance, mentally reviewing scenarios, or performing physical or mental rituals to neutralize their anxiety. Despite recognizing that these thoughts are irrational, individuals with harm OCD find it challenging to dismiss the obsessions, leading to significant distress and impairment in their daily lives. Having harm OCD does not mean a person is dangerous or likely to act on their intrusive thoughts.

Hit-and-Run

Hit-and-run OCD, also known as hit-and-run obsessive-compulsive disorder, is a subtype of OCD characterized by intrusive and distressing thoughts or obsessions related to causing harm or being involved in a hit-and-run accident. Individuals with hit-and-run OCD experience intense anxiety, guilt, and fear associated with the possibility of causing harm to others while driving. They may have intrusive thoughts about hitting pedestrians, cyclists, or other vehicles, even though there is no evidence or actual incidents to support these fears.

Hit-and-run obsessions can be accompanied by mental images or scenarios of accidents, leading to heightened anxiety and distress. Individuals with hit-and-run OCD may engage in various compulsive behaviors or rituals to prevent the feared harm, such as excessive checking of the surroundings, reviewing footage from dashboard cameras, avoiding certain driving routes or situations, or seeking reassurance from others about their driving. Despite recognizing that these fears are irrational, individuals with hit-and-run OCD find it challenging to dismiss the obsessions, leading to significant distress and impairment in their daily lives.

Intrusive Thoughts - (Pure-O)

Intrusive thoughts OCD, also known as pure-O OCD or purely obsessional OCD, is a subtype of OCD characterized by intrusive and distressing thoughts, images, or impulses that repeatedly enter a person's mind. The title "pure-O" is a misnomer as it leads one to believe that the individual experiences only obsessive doubt without performing any compulsions. It's important to note that having intrusive thoughts does not mean a person desires or intends to act on them. These thoughts are distressing and ego-dystonic, meaning they are inconsistent with a person's core values and intentions.

Individuals with Pure-O may engage in internal compulsions, such as mental rituals, reassurance seeking, rumination, worry, or avoidance behaviors, in response to these obsessions. Although the compulsions are not visible to others, they still play a role in maintaining the OCD cycle. However, these rituals often provide only temporary relief and can contribute to the persistence of the obsessions.

Here are some examples of obsessions commonly experienced in Pure-O:

1. Intrusive Thoughts: Individuals with Pure-O often experience intrusive thoughts that are distressing, unwanted, and often contradictory to their personal values. These thoughts can be violent, sexual, blasphemous, or socially unacceptable in nature. For example, someone might have repetitive thoughts of harming a loved one or engaging in inappropriate sexual behavior.

2. Doubt and Uncertainty: People with Pure-O often experience intense doubt and uncertainty about various aspects of their lives. They may constantly question their decisions, fear making irreversible mistakes, or doubt their own intentions or morality. This can lead to excessive rumination and mental analysis.

3. Existential or Philosophical Concerns: Some individuals with Pure-O may obsess over existential or philosophical questions, such as the meaning of life, the nature of reality, or the existence of a higher power. They may engage in prolonged introspection,

attempting to find definitive answers to these complex questions.

4. Relationship Obsessions: Pure-O can manifest as obsessions related to relationships, leading to doubts about romantic partners, friendships, or family members. Individuals may obsess over the authenticity of their relationships, fear losing someone's love or approval, or constantly question their partner's faithfulness.

5. Health and Disease Obsessions: People with Pure-O may experience intense anxiety and preoccupation with their health. They may obsess over perceived symptoms, worry about having a serious illness, or constantly seek reassurance from medical professionals. These obsessions can lead to excessive research of medical conditions and self-diagnosis.

6. Sexual Orientation or Identity Obsessions: Some individuals with Pure-O may obsess over their sexual orientation or gender identity, even when there is no evidence to support this doubt or uncertainty. These obsessions occur despite a history of healthy and fulfilling relationships with the preferred gender or no history of dysphoria with their gender identity. They may constantly question and analyze their attractions or engage in mental rituals to seek certainty.

Just Right

Just-right OCD, also known as just-right obsessive-compulsive disorder, is a subtype of OCD characterized by a need for symmetry, exactness, and a sense of completeness in one's actions or environment. Individuals with just-right OCD experience intrusive thoughts and discomfort when things feel "off" or not in a specific order, or out of alignment. They have an intense desire for things to be in a particular arrangement, position, or sequence that feels "just right."

The same need for things to feel "just right" can apply to a task or assignment. They may not be able to clearly identify what is wrong, but they must continue to revise their work until it feels "just right." Just right obsessive doubt can manifest in various aspects of their lives, including daily routines, organizing objects, or engaging in specific tasks.

Magical Thinking

Magical thinking OCD is a subtype of obsessive-compulsive disorder characterized by irrational beliefs that one's thoughts, words, or actions can influence events or have a magical impact on the world. Individuals with this obsession often engage in compulsive behaviors or rituals to prevent perceived negative consequences or to bring about desired outcomes.

Here are some examples of OCD magical thinking:

1. Superstitious Beliefs: People with magical thinking OCD may develop strong superstitious beliefs and

rituals. For example, they might believe that certain numbers are "lucky" or "unlucky" and feel compelled to perform specific actions or avoid certain behaviors based on these beliefs. They may engage in repetitive rituals, such as tapping objects a certain number of times or avoiding specific colors, to prevent bad luck or bring about good fortune.

2. Rituals to Prevent Harm: Individuals with magical thinking may believe that their thoughts or actions can cause harm to themselves or others. They may perform rituals to counteract these perceived harmful effects. For instance, they might feel the need to say specific phrases or perform specific actions repeatedly to prevent accidents, illness, or misfortune.

3. Thought-Action Fusion: People with magical thinking OCD may experience thought-action fusion, where they believe that having a particular thought is equivalent to actually carrying out the action. For example, they might believe that having a thought of harm or violence toward someone is equivalent to causing harm to that person. This can lead to extreme anxiety and the need to perform rituals or seek reassurance to alleviate their distress.

4. Avoidance of "Bad" Thoughts: Individuals with magical thinking OCD may engage in avoidance behaviors to prevent specific thoughts or images from occurring. They might avoid certain words,

places, or triggers that they associate with negative thoughts or potential harm. This avoidance can severely restrict their daily activities and social interactions.

5. Compulsive Prayer: Some individuals with magical thinking obsessions may engage in excessive praying or religious rituals. They might believe that their prayers can influence the outcome of events or prevent negative consequences. They may feel compelled to repeat prayers a specific number of times or engage in specific gestures to ensure their prayers are effective. It is important to note that these behaviors go far beyond what is typically expected of people who practice the religion or spiritual practice in question.

6. Magical Rituals for Control: People with OCD magical thinking may develop rituals or behaviors to gain a sense of control over uncertain or unpredictable events. They might perform specific actions, such as arranging objects in a certain order or following specific routines, believing that these behaviors will prevent negative outcomes or bring about desired results.

Perfectionism

Perfectionism OCD is characterized by an overwhelming need to achieve flawlessness or an intense fear of making mistakes. Individuals with this subtype of

OCD often set excessively high standards for themselves and are driven to perform repetitive behaviors to ensure perfection. It's important to note that perfectionism is a common trait among many individuals, but in the context of OCD, it becomes excessive, distressing, and time-consuming, significantly interfering with daily functioning.

Many common OCD obsessions can be the subject matter of perfection OCD. Examples include:

1. Symmetry and Order: People with perfectionistic obsessions may feel an intense need for things to be symmetrical or arranged in a specific order. They might spend excessive amounts of time organizing their belongings, aligning objects precisely, or adjusting items until they feel they are in perfect alignment.

2. Precision and Exactness: Some individuals with perfectionism-related OCD obsess over precision and exactness in their work or daily activities. They might repeatedly measure or count objects, align them meticulously, or spend excessive time on tasks to ensure everything is done precisely.

3. Fear of Making Mistakes: Those with perfectionism-related OCD may have an intense fear of making mistakes or overlooking details. They might engage in repetitive checking behaviors to ensure they have not made errors. For example, they may proofread a document multiple times, review emails excessively

before sending them, or constantly review their work for any perceived imperfections.

4. Intrusive Thoughts of Imperfection: Individuals with perfectionistic obsessions may experience intrusive thoughts that they are inherently flawed or imperfect. These thoughts can be distressing and cause significant anxiety. They may engage in repetitive mental rituals or seek reassurance from others to alleviate these intrusive thoughts.

5. Hoarding and Difficulty Discarding Items: Perfectionism can also manifest as an obsessive need to hold onto items for fear of needing them in the future or fear of discarding something important. This can lead to excessive clutter and difficulty letting go of possessions, even if they are no longer needed or have no practical value.

6. Excessive Rechecking: Perfectionism-related OCD can involve repetitive checking behaviors to ensure everything is done perfectly. This can include repeatedly reviewing tasks, revisiting completed work, or double-checking actions to make sure no mistakes have been made.

Relationship

Relationship OCD, also known as relationship-related obsessive-compulsive disorder, is a subtype of OCD that revolves around persistent doubts, obsessions, and anxiety about one's romantic or interpersonal relationships.

Individuals with relationship OCD experience intrusive thoughts and fears that cast doubt on the authenticity, compatibility, or fidelity of their relationship, even when there is no objective evidence to support these doubts. They may constantly seek reassurance from their partner, engage in excessive analysis and overthinking, or compulsively check their feelings and behaviors to ensure the relationship is "right" or "perfect."

Examples of relationship OCD might include repeatedly questioning one's love for a partner, obsessively checking communication records or social media activities of the partner for signs of infidelity, or constantly seeking reassurance from friends or family about the relationship's validity. These obsessive thoughts and compulsive behaviors can create significant distress and strain on the individual's relationship and overall well-being.

Scrupulosity/Religiosity

Scrupulosity OCD, also known as religiosity OCD or moral OCD, is a subtype of obsessive-compulsive disorder characterized by intrusive and distressing obsessions and fears related to religious or moral beliefs. Individuals with scrupulosity OCD experience intense anxiety, guilt, and fear of committing religious or moral transgressions, even when their actions are in line with their personal values and religious teachings. They may have intrusive thoughts or doubts about blasphemy, sin, or moral purity, leading to an excessive preoccupation with religious rituals, rules, or perfectionism.

Examples of scrupulosity OCD might include obsessive concerns about unintentionally committing sacrilegious acts, excessive worry about breaking religious rules or rituals, or a constant fear of having immoral thoughts. Individuals with scrupulosity OCD may engage in compulsive behaviors, such as excessive prayer, seeking reassurance from religious figures, confessing sins repeatedly, or engaging in rituals to "undo" perceived moral wrongdoings. Despite their best efforts, individuals with scrupulosity OCD often experience distress and doubt, as the obsessions continue to recur. It's important to note that scrupulosity OCD does not reflect an individual's true religious beliefs, but rather an exaggerated and distressing response to these beliefs.

Sexual Orientation

Sexual orientation OCD, also known as SO-OCD, is a subtype of OCD characterized by persistent and intrusive doubts, fears, and uncertainty about one's sexual orientation. Individuals with sexual orientation OCD experience distressing thoughts and obsessions related to their sexual identity, causing significant anxiety and confusion. They may question their sexual attractions and constantly seek reassurance or engage in mental rituals to confirm their sexual orientation.

Examples of sexual orientation OCD might include obsessive thoughts such as "What if I'm actually attracted to the same (or different) sex?" or "What if I'm not really heterosexual (gay or bisexual)?" These thoughts can lead to an excessive analysis of past experiences or behaviors, seeking external validation, or avoiding situations that trigger uncertainty about one's sexual orientation. It's important to note that sexual orientation OCD is not reflective of an individual's actual sexual orientation, but rather a manifestation of OCD that causes distress and interferes with daily functioning.

Somatic

Somatic OCD, also known as illness anxiety disorder or health anxiety, is a subtype of OCD characterized by excessive worry and preoccupation with having a serious medical condition. Individuals with somatic OCD often interpret normal bodily sensations as signs of a severe illness, leading to distress and impairment in daily functioning. Here are some examples of somatic OCD obsessions. It's important to note that these examples represent some common obsessions associated with somatic OCD. However, experiences with OCD can vary, and the obsessions and compulsions can take various forms.

1. Fear of Cancer: Individuals with somatic OCD may develop an intense fear of developing cancer. They may obsessively research symptoms, risk factors, and medical articles related to cancer. Even minor bodily changes, such as a small bump or a headache,

can trigger intense anxiety and lead to frequent doctor visits or medical tests.

2. Hypochondria: Some individuals with somatic OCD exhibit hypochondriacal tendencies. They constantly worry about having various diseases or medical conditions. They might excessively monitor their body for any perceived abnormalities, seeking reassurance from doctors or searching the internet for symptoms.

3. Hyperawareness of Bodily Sensations: People with somatic OCD often become hyperaware of their bodily sensations. They may interpret normal bodily functions, such as heart palpitations, muscle twitches, or digestive noises, as signs of a serious medical issue. This hyperfocus on bodily sensations can be distressing and lead to frequent doctor visits or seeking constant reassurance.

4. Compulsive Checking: Individuals with somatic OCD may engage in compulsive checking behaviors related to their health. They might frequently measure their vital signs, such as blood pressure or heart rate, to ensure they are within normal ranges. They may also repeatedly examine their body for any unusual lumps or bumps, even if they have been assured by medical professionals that they are healthy.

5. Fear of Contamination: Some individuals with somatic OCD may develop a fear of contamination by germs or harmful substances. They might obsessively wash their hands or sanitize their surroundings, believing that it will prevent them from acquiring a serious illness.

6. Repeated Medical Tests: People with somatic OCD may undergo unnecessary medical tests or procedures, seeking reassurance about their health. They might visit multiple doctors or specialists to receive second or third opinions, despite consistently being told they are healthy.

Common Compulsions

Individuals with OCD are caught in a loop beginning with obsessive doubt that leads to feelings of distress. To relieve feelings of distress, people with OCD engage in compulsions or rituals. Here is a review of some common types of compulsions:

Avoidance

The OCD compulsion of avoidance involves deliberately avoiding certain situations, objects, places, or thoughts to reduce anxiety or prevent triggering obsessions. Individuals with this compulsion engage in avoidance behaviors to manage their distress and prevent the discomfort associated with their obsessive thoughts. Here are some examples of avoidance behaviors in OCD:

1. Environmental Avoidance: Individuals may avoid specific environments or places that they associate with their obsessions. For example, someone with contamination obsessions might avoid public restrooms, crowded areas, or places they perceive as dirty. Similarly, a person with intrusive thoughts about violence or harm may avoid locations that remind them of those thoughts, such as certain streets or alleys.

2. Social Avoidance: People with OCD may engage in social avoidance to prevent triggering their obsessions or to avoid situations that may induce anxiety. They might avoid social events, parties, or gatherings where they fear they might experience distressing thoughts or be unable to perform their compulsions. This can lead to isolation and withdrawal from social activities.

3. Thought Avoidance: Some individuals attempt to avoid or suppress certain thoughts or images associated with their obsessions. They may distract themselves or engage in mental rituals to block out unwanted thoughts. For example, a person with intrusive thoughts of violence might deliberately redirect their attention or engage in repetitive mental activities to prevent those thoughts from occurring.

4. Task Avoidance: OCD-related avoidance can involve avoiding specific tasks or activities that trigger anxiety or are associated with obsessive

thoughts. For instance, someone with contamination obsessions might avoid handling certain objects, refuse to touch doorknobs, or avoid tasks that require contact with potentially "contaminated" surfaces.

5. Avoiding Triggers: Individuals may actively avoid triggers or situations that they associate with their obsessions. This can include avoiding specific people, books, movies, or television shows that they believe will trigger distressing thoughts or worsen their obsessions. They might also avoid reading or hearing news related to their fears or anxieties.

6. Avoidance of Uncertainty: Some people with OCD engage in avoidance behaviors to reduce uncertainty and anxiety. They may avoid making decisions or acting if they cannot guarantee a specific outcome or if they fear making a mistake. This can lead to excessive indecisiveness, procrastination, or avoidance of situations that involve uncertainty.

It's important to note that while avoidance provides temporary relief, it reinforces the cycle of OCD by maintaining anxiety and preventing individuals from learning that their feared outcomes are unlikely to occur.

Checking

Checking is a common compulsion associated with OCD. It involves repetitive and excessive behaviors aimed at ensuring that something is safe, secure, or free from harm. Individuals with checking compulsions often experience intense fear or doubt, and performing the checking behavior temporarily alleviates their anxiety. However, the relief is short-lived, leading to a cycle of repeated checking. This behavior can consume a significant amount of time and interfere with daily functioning.

Examples of checking compulsions include:

1. Checking locks: Frequently verifying that doors, windows, or car locks are properly secured to prevent intruders or accidents.

2. Checking appliances: Repeatedly ensuring that the stove, oven, or electrical devices are turned off to avoid potential fires or hazards.

3. Checking personal belongings: Continuously checking bags, wallets, or pockets to confirm that essential items such as identification, money, or keys are present.

4. Checking for safety: Repeatedly examining the environment for potential dangers or hazards, such as checking for slippery surfaces, sharp objects, or potential sources of contamination.

5. Checking health: Frequent body checks, such as examining the skin for signs of illness, checking vital signs repeatedly, or constantly monitoring for physical symptoms, even when there is no objective evidence of any health issue.

6. Checking documents: Repeatedly reviewing or rereading documents, such as emails, text messages, or written materials, to ensure accuracy or prevent mistakes.

7. Checking for mistakes: Double or triple-checking completed tasks or assignments for errors, such as proofreading extensively or reviewing work multiple times before submitting it.

8. Checking for Accidents: This involves repeatedly checking for signs of accidents or potential harm. For instance, an individual may repeatedly check if they ran over someone while driving, even though they know it is highly unlikely or impossible.

These are just a few examples of the checking obsession in OCD. It's important to note that the severity and specific manifestations of OCD can vary from person to person. OCD is a complex condition, and it often requires professional help for proper diagnosis and treatment.

Cleaning

Cleaning compulsions are common manifestations of OCD. Individuals with this compulsion engage in repetitive and excessive behaviors related to cleanliness, hygiene, or the removal of perceived contaminants. These compulsions are driven by an intense fear of contamination or the desire to prevent harm. Although the actions provide temporary relief, the anxiety and obsessions tend to resurface, leading to a cycle of repetitive washing and cleaning.

Examples of washing and cleaning compulsions include:

1. Excessive handwashing: Frequent and prolonged washing of hands with soap and water, often accompanied by specific rituals or patterns, such as scrubbing each finger individually or washing for a certain duration.

2. Repetitive bathing or showering: Engaging in multiple showers or baths within a short period or taking excessively long showers to achieve a perceived sense of cleanliness.

3. Cleaning rituals: Spending an excessive amount of time cleaning and disinfecting surfaces, objects, or personal belongings, such as wiping down countertops, doorknobs, or electronic devices repeatedly.

4. Excessive laundry: Repeatedly washing and rewashing clothes, bedding, or towels due to a persistent fear of contamination or dirtiness.

5. Avoidance of "contaminated" items: Discarding or avoiding objects that are perceived as contaminated, such as avoiding public restrooms, using disposable utensils, or replacing items frequently to ensure cleanliness.

6. Excessive grooming or oral hygiene: Spending excessive time on grooming activities, such as brushing teeth repeatedly, flossing excessively, or

engaging in prolonged personal care routines to achieve a sense of cleanliness.

7. Compulsive cleaning of body parts: Repeatedly cleaning specific body parts, such as washing hands excessively, scrubbing skin excessively, or cleaning nails repeatedly to eliminate perceived contamination.

Counting

Counting and mathematical compulsions are a type of compulsive behavior commonly observed in OCD. Individuals with counting and mathematical compulsions often feel a strong urge to count, perform calculations, or engage in repetitive numerical rituals. These compulsions are driven by a need for certainty, symmetry, or to neutralize intrusive thoughts, and they temporarily alleviate anxiety but perpetuate the OCD cycle.

Examples of counting and mathematical compulsions include:

1. Counting objects: Feeling compelled to count objects, such as steps, tiles, or items in a room, repeatedly and precisely, to achieve a specific number or pattern.

2. Numerical patterns: Engaging in rituals based on specific numerical patterns or sequences, such as counting in even numbers, counting by intervals, or reciting numbers in a particular order.

3. Repeating numbers: Repeating numbers or numerical sequences in the mind or out loud to reduce anxiety or prevent harm. This can involve repeating phone numbers, addresses, or numerical patterns multiple times.

4. Mathematical calculations: Frequently performing calculations, such as adding, subtracting, multiplying, or dividing numbers, to neutralize intrusive thoughts or reduce uncertainty.

5. Time-related rituals: Compulsively checking and calculating time, setting alarms or reminders, or adhering to strict schedules or routines to maintain order and alleviate anxiety.

6. Symmetry-based counting: Engaging in counting rituals to achieve symmetry or balance, such as counting objects on one side of a room and then counting an equal number on the other side.

7. Compulsive number placement: Rearranging or aligning objects to create numerical patterns or to ensure specific numerical relationships are maintained.

8. Checking and rechecking calculations: Repeatedly checking and recalculating numbers or mathematical equations to ensure accuracy and prevent perceived mistakes.

Ordering

Ordering compulsions are a type of OCD compulsion characterized by a strong need for things to be arranged in a particular order, symmetry, or alignment. Individuals with ordering compulsions often feel a sense of discomfort or anxiety when items are not organized according to their desired pattern. They engage in repetitive and ritualistic behaviors to create a sense of order and control.

Examples of ordering compulsions include:

1. Arranging objects: Spending excessive time arranging objects, such as books, items on shelves, or personal belongings, in a specific order, based on criteria like size, color, or specific patterns.

2. Symmetry rituals: Ensuring that objects are perfectly balanced and symmetrical by repeatedly adjusting and aligning them until they feel "just right." This may involve aligning items at precise angles or ensuring that objects are evenly spaced.

3. Repeating actions: Repeating actions or movements until they are performed symmetrically or evenly, such as taking an equal number of steps with each foot or touching objects an equal number of times with each hand.

4. Numerical rituals: Engaging in rituals based on specific numerical patterns, such as counting or arranging items in multiples or specific sequences

(e.g., counting to a certain number, touching objects a specific number of times).

5. Compulsive organizing: Spending excessive time organizing digital files, folders, or computer desktops to ensure a particular order or structure is maintained.

6. Reordering or redoing tasks: Feeling compelled to redo tasks or activities if they are not performed in the "correct" order or sequence, even if the original outcome was acceptable.

7. Hoarding to maintain order: Accumulating or hoarding items due to a fear of disorder or a belief that keeping items will prevent chaos or disruption.

Reassurance Seeking

The OCD compulsion of reassurance-seeking involves seeking repeated assurance or validation from others to alleviate anxiety or doubt associated with obsessive thoughts or fears. Individuals with this compulsion often feel compelled to seek reassurance to temporarily reduce their anxiety, even though it provides only short-term relief. Here are some examples of reassurance-seeking behaviors in OCD:

1. Seeking Reassurance from Loved Ones: Individuals may repeatedly seek reassurance from family members, friends, or romantic partners. For example, they might ask their loved ones repeatedly if they are

still loved or if they have done something wrong. They may seek reassurance about their appearance, intelligence, or perceived flaws.

2. Repeatedly Asking for Opinions or Feedback: People with reassurance-seeking compulsions may repeatedly ask for opinions or feedback on their decisions, actions, or performance. They might seek reassurance that they have completed a task correctly, that their work is satisfactory, or that they have made the right choice. They may ask for repeated confirmation to alleviate doubts or uncertainties.

3. Checking with Professionals: Individuals with OCD may frequently seek reassurance from professionals, such as doctors, therapists, or experts, about their health, symptoms, or concerns. They might seek multiple medical opinions, request additional tests or evaluations, or constantly ask for reassurance that they are not at risk of a particular illness or condition.

4. Internet Reassurance-Seeking: With the prevalence of online information, people with reassurance-seeking compulsions may spend excessive amounts of time researching and seeking reassurance on the Internet. They might search for medical information, browse forums, or seek confirmation from online communities to validate their concerns or alleviate anxiety.

5. Reviewing Past Conversations or Events: Reassurance-seeking can involve repeatedly reviewing past conversations, messages, or events to seek reassurance that they haven't said or done something wrong. Individuals may obsessively analyze their interactions, looking for any signs of potential mistakes or negative consequences.

6. Mental Reassurance-Seeking: Some individuals engage in mental compulsions to seek reassurance. They might repetitively review their thoughts or mental images, seeking certainty that they do not align with their fears or obsessions. They may mentally repeat phrases or perform mental rituals to reassure themselves and temporarily reduce anxiety.

Repetitive Thoughts

Worry and rumination are two common types of repetitive thought compulsions associated with OCD. Worry and rumination compulsions involve excessive and repetitive thinking, analyzing, or reviewing of the obsessions, often driven by a need for certainty, reassurance, or to prevent perceived harm.

Worry is a compulsion characterized by excessive and persistent concerns about potential future events, negative outcomes, or uncertainties. It involves a continuous cycle of anxious thoughts and attempts to solve or prevent the feared situations. Worry is an attempt to gain control and reduce anxiety, but it ultimately reinforces the belief that the feared outcomes are significant and need constant attention and that uncertainty is dangerous or unbearable.

Rumination, on the other hand, involves repetitive and intrusive thoughts or mental replaying of past events, often focused on negative experiences, mistakes, or regrets. It is an intense fixation on specific thoughts or memories, with a compulsion to analyze and search for answers, meaning, or resolution. Rumination can be fueled by a desire for certainty, self-criticism, or a need to prevent future errors.

Examples of worry and rumination compulsions include:

1. Excessive planning and overthinking: Spending excessive time and mental energy planning for potential negative outcomes or repeatedly going over details to ensure everything is accounted for.

2. Mental rehearsal: Engaging in repetitive mental rehearsals or simulations of future events to mentally prepare for possible scenarios or to prevent harm or mistakes.

3. Seeking reassurance: Seeking reassurance from others or repeatedly asking for advice or opinions to alleviate uncertainty or gain confirmation of safety or correctness.

4. Constant analyzing and reviewing: Engaging in repetitive mental reviewing of past events, conversations, or decisions, to identify what went

wrong or seeking reassurance that no harm was caused.

5. Hypervigilance and monitoring: Constantly monitoring one's thoughts, feelings, or physical sensations for signs of danger, discomfort, or mistakes, with a compulsion to seek reassurance or alleviate anxiety.

6. Endless "what if" scenarios: Generating and analyzing countless hypothetical situations, trying to anticipate and prevent negative outcomes or worst-case scenarios.

7. Repeated checking or fact-checking: Engaging in excessive fact-checking, researching, or seeking information to verify or disprove obsessions or worries.

Scrupulosity/Morality

Compulsions associated with scrupulosity/morality OCD, also known as religiosity OCD, involve repetitive behaviors or rituals driven by excessive concerns about religious or moral purity, fear of committing sins, or worries about blasphemy. These compulsions are typically performed to alleviate distress, but they can become time-consuming, mentally exhausting, and significantly impact daily functioning.

Examples of compulsions in scrupulosity/morality OCD include:

1. Excessive prayer or religious rituals: Engaging in repetitive prayer or religious rituals, beyond what is considered customary, to seek forgiveness, ward off perceived sins, or obtain reassurance of moral purity.

2. Confession or reassurance-seeking: Frequent confession of perceived sins or seeking reassurance from religious authorities, family members, or friends about moral conduct, religious beliefs, or fears of committing blasphemy.

3. Excessive moral self-analysis: Constantly analyzing thoughts, motives, or actions to determine if they are morally acceptable, often seeking certainty or reassurance that one's behavior aligns with religious or moral standards.

4. Avoidance of religious triggers: Avoiding situations, places, or activities that trigger distressing religious or moral obsessions, such as religious services, religious texts, or discussions about controversial moral topics.

5. Mental rituals or prayers: Engaging in internal mental rituals, such as repeating specific prayers, seeking mental reassurance, or mentally reviewing moral conduct to neutralize intrusive thoughts or alleviate guilt.

6. Excessive reading or studying religious texts: Spending excessive time studying religious texts, seeking absolute clarity on religious or moral

principles, or repeatedly reviewing specific passages to alleviate doubt or prevent perceived moral transgressions.

7. Excessive charitable acts: Engaging in excessive or ritualistic acts of charity or self-sacrifice to compensate for perceived moral failings or to seek reassurance of moral righteousness.

8. Moral perfectionism: Setting excessively high moral standards for oneself and striving for perfection in moral conduct, constantly monitoring behavior for any perceived shortcomings.

Somatic

OCD compulsions related to somatic issues are characterized by excessive preoccupation with and repetitive behaviors surrounding physical sensations, bodily functions, or health concerns. Individuals with this subtype of OCD often have intense fears or obsessions about having a serious illness or bodily dysfunction. These fears can lead to compulsive behaviors aimed at seeking reassurance, alleviating anxiety, or preventing perceived harm.

Examples of OCD compulsions related to somatic issues include:

1. Checking and monitoring: Engaging in frequent checking or monitoring of bodily functions, such as repeatedly checking pulse rate, body temperature, or

breathing patterns, to ensure they are within normal ranges.

2. Medical reassurance-seeking: Seeking repeated medical consultations, second opinions, or medical tests to alleviate fears of having a serious illness, despite reassurances from healthcare professionals.

3. Excessive researching: Spending excessive time researching symptoms, medical conditions, or potential illnesses, often seeking information to confirm or disprove health-related obsessions.

4. Compulsive body checking: Frequently examining the body for signs of illness, abnormalities, or physical sensations, and seeking reassurance by comparing oneself to others or previous experiences.

5. Self-diagnosis: Constantly evaluating and diagnosing oneself based on perceived symptoms or bodily sensations, often seeking validation or reassurance from online sources or self-help materials.

6. Avoidance behaviors: Avoiding situations or activities believed to trigger or worsen somatic symptoms or fears of illness, such as avoiding exercise, specific foods, or social interactions.

7. Repeated hygiene rituals: Engaging in excessive hygiene behaviors, such as excessive handwashing or disinfecting, to prevent the spread of perceived

contaminants or to alleviate fears of contracting illnesses.

8. Reassurance-seeking from others: Frequently seeking reassurance or validation from family members, friends, or online communities regarding health concerns, symptoms, or bodily sensations.

9. Imaginal exposure rituals: Engaging in mental rituals or imaginal exposures to confront and "test" fears of illness, often involving vividly imagining worst-case scenarios or bodily malfunctions.

Factors That Can Affect Treatment

Family Accommodation and Intolerance

The distress and impairment associated with OCD affects not only the person with the disorder but also the people who love and care about the affected person. Family units can be particularly impacted by OCD and family members often begin to accommodate OCD in several ways. Family accommodation can look like changing family routines to make time for the rituals involved in OCD, facilitating avoidance, or participating in compulsions to reduce the emotional distress of the family member with OCD. Parents may engage in excessive handwashing to alleviate their child's concerns about germs or may give excessive reassurance that the doors are locked.

These behaviors are often well-intentioned, stemming from a desire to lessen the distress experienced by the OCD sufferer or reflecting an effort to help their loved one function more smoothly in his/her daily life. However, research has demonstrated that family accommodation is associated with increases in OCD symptom severity, increased functional impairment due to OCD, and decreased response to treatment (Wu et al., 2016). Family accommodation prevents individuals with OCD from facing their feared situations, testing their OCD beliefs, and developing more adaptive strategies for managing distress and uncertainty. Studies have shown that decreases in family accommodation precede decreases in OCD symptom severity and functional impairment (Piacentini et al., 2011).

An important part of treatment for patients with friends or family members who may engage in these accommodating behaviors is providing education about how this negatively impacts OCD and treatment. The patient and therapist should work together to identify ways that friends and family members may be unintentionally facilitating their obsessions and compulsions and discuss how to address this with the patient's loved ones. As it is the patient him/herself who must engage in treatment to recover from OCD, this can be an important step towards developing the patient's autonomy and increasing self-efficacy beliefs.

On the other end of the spectrum, rather than accommodating their loved one's OCD, some families demonstrate extreme intolerance of their loved one's OCD. Family intolerance may involve verbally berating the individual for their inability to overcome or suppress their OCD symptoms, treating them coldly or harshly, or demanding that they "just stop it!" While navigating the distress and disruption caused by OCD can be frustrating for family members, this intolerance is counterproductive and destructive. These interactions often heighten the anxiety and distress experienced by people with OCD and may increase the severity of their symptoms. Additionally, many people with OCD experience considerable shame related to their OCD and struggle mightily against it. Recovering from OCD and fully engaging in effective treatment for OCD requires determination, will, and strength. People with OCD need loving support and encouragement from their loved ones as they reclaim control of their lives.

Accommodon't (TM)

One of the most difficult things for a family member, loved one, or caregiver is to refrain from accommodating compulsions. For purposes of clarity, I will refer to them all as "loved ones." A loved one's desire to accommodate emanates from the desire to be helpful. An individual with OCD's obsessive doubt causes a great deal of distress. As a result, they engage in compulsions to reduce their distress. They often find it necessary to recruit their loved ones into the compulsive behavior to attain ultimate distress reduction.

For example, an individual who suffers from contamination OCD may fear that if they have been out of the house in public, their hands, body, shoes, and clothes may be contaminated. Once they return home, they will spread that contamination all around their house unless they leave their shoes at the door, place their clothes in the wash, and immediately shower. This compulsive cleaning temporarily reduces their distress, but it only works if they live alone. If there are other members of the household then the individual with OCD must convince everyone in the house to follow the same rules or they, too will spread contamination upon returning home.

Often, loved ones will comply and accommodate the request because they believe that noncompliance means that they are responsible for increasing their loved one's distress. Since they have an honest desire to help their loved one, they reason that if they make some adjustments to their routine, then they are helping their loved one by reducing their distress. The problem is that this accommodation is a compulsive activity, and it reinforces the negative OCD cycle. If the individual with OCD starts treatment, then all accommodation must stop. If accommodation continues, all the gains made in therapy are erased as soon as the patient returns home. Paradoxically, the loved one's desire to help the patient directly harms the patient.

But how can a loved one stop accommodating without coming across as mean-spirited and uncaring? This is a challenge I face in most cases where a patient interfaces with someone who accommodates them. As a result, I created the Accommodon't [(TM)] process. It reinforces the learning that the patient is gaining in therapy and allows for a meaningful, compassionate response from the loved one. It is easy to remember because it is based on the five vowels, A, E, I, O, U.

Here is how it works. First, I introduce the process to both the patient and the loved ones by explaining why we use it and then reviewing each step. We use the process because, for treatment to be effective, all outside sources of accommodation must stop while the patient learns how to manage their own obsessive thoughts without performing compulsions. When a patient performs compulsions or is accommodated, they are no longer able to face their doubt, which is an essential part of the response-prevention phase of exposure and response prevention (ERP) therapy, which will be discussed in detail in a later chapter. The patient is striving for Inhibitory Learning as part of their treatment process. This requires that they learn about OCD, face the distress they feel from their obsessive doubt, and recognize that they can tolerate it. They also discover that the bad things they expect don't necessarily happen or at least are only possibilities, not probabilities.

Therefore, if a patient seeks to recruit a loved one to accommodate them, the loved one can now effectively engage in the Accommodon't ^(TM) process. The process has 5 steps that are easy to remember because they are based on the vowels A, E, I, O and U.

A - "A" stands for Acknowledge. The loved one must acknowledge what the patient wants and why they want it. *"I understand that you want me to take my shoes off and wash my hands when I return home so that I do not spread contamination."*

E - "E" stands for Explain. Explain that the patient's request sounds like a request for accommodation. *"Do you realize that your request sounds like an OCD accommodation? Are you having obsessive doubts?"*

I - "I" stands for I'm sorry. *"I'm sorry but you know that I can't accommodate your request, or I will actually be interfering with your recovery by making OCD stronger."*

O - "O" stands for Options. *"Let's talk about some options we have to help you address the obsessive doubt and help you beat OCD."*

U - "U" stands for Understanding. In this part of the process, the loved one confirms the agreed-upon process from the options discussion. *"So we are in agreement that the next time you want me to take my shoes off and wash my hands when I come home, I will ..."*

Let's look at an example. Sarah is 14 years old and lives at home with her mother. Sarah has contamination OCD, specifically eating-related. She engages in the compulsion of checking. Every time Sarah enters the kitchen to eat something, she must first ask her mother if the plate she is using is clean, if the glass she plans to drink from is safe to use, and whether her mother used any cleaning products on the kitchen countertops. Every time, Sarah's mother reassures her that the dishes are clean and safe. She also had to stop properly cleaning the kitchen so that Sarah would not see any cleaning products being used. Ironically, the decision not to use appropriate cleaning products in the kitchen makes the kitchen less clean and less safe.

Sarah began ERP treatment for her OCD, and I explained that her mother can no longer accommodate her. I then explained the Accommodon't [TM] process. When they got home, the conversation went as follows:

Sarah: Mom, are these dishes clean and safe to eat from?

Mom: I understand that you are concerned whether the dishes are clean and safe to eat from because you don't want to get contaminated.

Sarah: That's right. So, can you tell me?

Mom: Do you realize that your request sounds like you want me to accommodate your OCD? Are you having obsessive doubts?

Sarah: Yes. Please just tell me this once. I promise I won't keep asking. I just need to know for sure.

Mom: I'm sorry but you know that I can't accommodate your request, or I will actually be undoing the work you are doing in therapy and making your OCD worse.

Sarah: I know, but pleeease just answer this one last time. I just need to know.

Mom: Let's talk about some options we have that can help address your obsessive doubt while also helping you beat your OCD.

Sarah: But how?

Mom: Well, suppose we do this. You ask the same questions for reassurance every time you enter the kitchen. Why don't you get a pad and write them down? I will answer them one last time for you and you write the answers on the pad next to each question. Then, the next time you ask me, I will simply refer you to the pad, but I will no longer answer any question on the pad.

Sarah: Well, I guess we could try.

Mom: So, are we in agreement that you are going to write out all your questions on the pad and I will answer them one last time? You will write down the answer and the next time you ask me a question on the pad, I will refer you to the pad. Any new questions and answers will be added to the pad.

Sarah: Yes.

It is important that the options portion of the process is an interactive discussion between the parties when needed. Options must be agreed upon, not imposed. Initially, this can take some work and creativity but after some practice, it becomes much easier.

Things Not to Say

When a person meets someone with OCD who is suffering from obvious obsessive doubt and related compulsions, it can be frustrating for both parties. It is important to remember that OCD is a mental disorder that requires professional treatment. Their desire to be free from OCD outweighs your desire to not have to witness them performing compulsions. You may interact with them for a short while, but they deal with OCD every hour of every day. It is important that when interacting with someone with OCD, you be supportive, non-judgmental, and compassionate. Offering acknowledgment and understanding while supporting the person to seek professional help is the best way to lead to their well-being and recovery.

The following is a list of some of the most common things people say to someone with OCD that are both counterproductive and condescending. These things may make the speaker feel better, but they make the person with OCD feel worse.

1. "I'm sure it can't be that big of a deal." It *is* a big deal to them. At times, the obsessive doubt can feel like torture. This statement is dismissive and condescending. It can make the person with OCD feel as if their struggles are neither valid nor important and can discourage them from seeking help.

2. "If you were really contaminated, do you think I would sleep next to you?" This is dismissive and can make the person with OCD feel small and ashamed. OCD is not logical and trying to address it with something that is logical to you is not helpful for them.

3. "Just relax and stop worrying so much." OCD is not simply a matter of excessive worrying that can be resolved by relaxation techniques. In fact, the person already engages in compulsions to try to relax. Don't you think they would relax if they could? OCD is a complex mental health condition that requires professional treatment.

4. "You're out of your mind! You're as crazy as your mother!" Criticism and blame do nothing but make the person with OCD feel guilt and shame. They are already probably struggling with beliefs about why

they have OCD. Adding to feelings that bring them down is cruel.

5. "Why don't you just stop doing those rituals?" It's essential to recognize that OCD rituals serve as coping mechanisms. Asking them to stop these rituals without understanding the underlying anxiety and compulsions may trivialize their experiences.

6. "You're just being too picky or perfectionistic." OCD is not about being overly detail-oriented or seeking perfection. It involves intrusive thoughts and uncontrollable urges that can significantly impact a person's daily life and cause distress.

7. "I'm a little OCD too; I like to keep things tidy." Using the term "OCD" casually or to describe personal preferences minimizes the severity and complexity of the disorder. It's important to distinguish between preferences and the distressing nature of OCD symptoms.

8. "Why don't you try not thinking about it?" Instructing someone with OCD to stop thinking about their obsessions is not helpful. The thoughts are involuntary, and attempting to suppress them can often worsen anxiety and reinforce obsessions.

Instead of the above, try saying: "I am concerned that you are exhibiting some obsessive and compulsive behaviors resembling OCD. Can I support you in finding a professional with whom you can speak? It may help you feel better."

Why Seek Treatment?

One of the most important reasons for seeking treatment for OCD is that the treatment works. There is strong evidence that treatment with exposure and response prevention (ERP) is effective for reducing the obsessions and compulsions and increasing well-being and functioning across multiple domains (Craske et al., 2014; Deacon & Abramowitz, 2004; Ludvik et al., 2015). ERP is the gold standard for treating OCD.

Helping patients identify reasons for engaging in therapy is key to building motivation for treatment. Questions like *"What has OCD caused you to miss out on?"* and *"How has it impacted your relationships, your friends and family, your self-esteem, and sense of identity?"* enables clients to consider the negative impact of OCD on their lives. Completing a cost-benefit analysis of engaging in treatment increases patients' motivation for treatment by highlighting the potential benefits of engaging in treatment and the cons of not engaging in treatment, while also realistically addressing the cons of treatment and the benefits of not participating in treatment (i.e., not having to face fears, costs of therapy). For many patients, OCD has significantly interfered with their lives and building patients 'beliefs in their ability to recover from OCD while highlighting what they stand to gain in their recovery can motivate them to fully commit to treatment.

Treatment Motivators

When individuals with OCD go untreated, they may face various challenges that can significantly impact their lives. Having OCD causes distress, but, for some people, the distress is seemingly worse when they imagine getting treatment. If a person is not motivated to participate in treatment, their chances of success are minimal. My understanding of treatment motivators closely follows the work of a leading authority in the field of OCD treatment, Jonathan Grayson, PhD in his book "Freedom from Obsessive-Compulsive Disorder (Grayson, 2003, 2014)". Here's what has worked best for patients in my clinical practice.

I work with my patients to evaluate their readiness for treatment. I do not try to convince or coerce them; I simply bring the realities of OCD and its impacts into focus using the Socratic method. The goal is for the patient to become clear about their own experiences and desires. I find it helpful if they use a scale of -5 to +5 to rate the benefit of remaining in a certain position versus being relieved of the situation. A rating of -5 means that the situation is not desirable at all and a +5 means the situation is highly desirable.

OCD as relates to self

Statements	Explain	Rating of staying in this position	Rating if you were relieved of this situation
Consider how much time in a day is devoted to OCD obsessions and compulsions.			
Consider the level of distress you feel when dealing with OCD.			
Consider the things you have missed out on or avoided because of OCD.			
Consider how you have felt around others due to your OCD.			
Consider how you feel about having OCD.			
Consider employment-related issues due to OCD.			
Consider financial issues related to OCD.			

OCD as relates to others

Statements	Explain	Rating of staying in this position	Rating if you were relieved of this situation
Consider whether you have asked others to accommodate your OCD.			
Consider OCD's impact on other's ability to spend time with you and share in your life.			
Consider how your reaction to OCD may have impacted others.			
Consider whether your OCD has impacted others by making them late to, or miss events all together.			
Consider what monetary impact your OCD may have had on others.			

Common Treatment Mistakes

OCD is unique and its diagnosis and treatment can be unlike other mental health disorders. One of the biggest reasons for the following treatment mistakes is that many graduate mental health programs, whether they are programs training mental health counselors, psychologists, or psychiatrists don't spend much, if any, time teaching OCD. I know that my graduate training did not cover it and I have interviewed many other mental health professionals who report the same. I started learning about OCD after I was licensed, and I had to seek out this knowledge on my own. Now, I spend part of my time teaching other mental health providers what I have learned.

Effective treatment of OCD involves more than teaching relaxation techniques, or helping patients think more rationally, or trying to force behavior change. ERP is a comprehensive treatment approach that educates patients about the nature of their OCD, helps them understand how their obsessions and compulsions trap them in the OCD cycle, and gives them tools to face their obsessions without engaging in compulsions. ERP is effective because inhibitory learning allows patients to test their OCD beliefs, learn new meanings and beliefs for OCD triggers, and increase their ability to access these new beliefs in a variety of different environments. ERP helps patients learn that anxiety, distress, and uncertainty are inevitable, universal, and not inherently harmful. Participating in exposures allows patients to develop skills for tolerating this distress and uncertainty.

Let's look at some common treatment mistakes:

Misdiagnosis

Accurate diagnosis of OCD is achieved through clinical interviews (e.g. the Structured Clinical Interview for DSM-V; SCID-V) and the use of OCD-specific assessment tools like the Yale-Brown Obsessive-Compulsive Scale (Y-BOCS) and the Children's Yale-Brown Obsessive-Compulsive Scale (CY-BOCS). A practitioner who is not trained in OCD may not even think to conduct these assessments because OCD is not on their radar. Misdiagnosis prevents patients from receiving proper treatment. OCD is often misdiagnosed as generalized anxiety disorder or disregarded as "normal" worries. Some types of OCD can be especially challenging, even for an OCD expert to diagnose. For example, OCD related to sexual orientation may be misdiagnosed as denial or difficulty embracing an identity, rather than understood as ego-dystonic obsessions and compulsions.

Co-occurring Disorders

Overlooking co-occurring mental health conditions can lead to ineffective treatment approaches. Proper assessment and accurate diagnoses are vital to developing an appropriate treatment plan. In my experience, many OCD patients may also suffer from unresolved trauma, generalized anxiety, or are on the autism spectrum. I have found that it is important to treat these co-occurring disorders first, or at least incorporate them into the treatment plan, or they can block the effectiveness of OCD therapy.

Relaxation Training

Another common treatment mistake is the belief that OCD can be treated by teaching the patient calming or relaxation techniques. When therapists teach patients relaxation techniques for OCD, it communicates to patients that if they could simply relax more easily their OCD would subside. This is untrue, as relaxation techniques often become additional compulsions for people with OCD. While there may be a place for these techniques within a comprehensive treatment regimen for OCD, it is only one component in the therapist's treatment toolbox. The main evidence-based treatment for OCD is ERP which is based on exposing the patient to obsessive thoughts and working towards inhibitory learning. This is quite the opposite of relaxation techniques in that effective therapy relies upon the intentional triggering of distress.

Talk Therapy

Talk therapy can be very effective in treating many mental health disorders. It helps patients identify and correct thought errors and cognitive distortions. This can be immensely helpful for many psychological disorders, but not for OCD. It is problematic for a therapist to rely on talk therapy to treat OCD. To be effective, talk therapy requires patients to think and respond logically. The obsessions and intrusive thoughts that characterize OCD are not cognitive distortions or thought errors; rather, they are OCD beliefs that are not logical and do not respond to reason. This cannot be overstated. Many patients understand this and acknowledge that their OCD beliefs are not true despite how real and distressing they feel. Simply helping patients to identify more reasonable thoughts is not enough to overcome obsessions and compulsions. If a person with OCD could reason their way out of OCD, they would do so.

Talk therapy also helps people to estimate risk more effectively. A common feature of depression and anxiety disorders is the tendency to overestimate the probability of failure or negative events. Talk therapy can be helpful for these disorders by teaching patients to challenge these distortions and replace them with more realistic thoughts. This is not sufficient for OCD, which thrives on uncertainty. Effective treatment for OCD requires patients to confront the reality that things happen sometimes, and we don't have nearly as much control over events in our lives as we like to think that we do. As such, successful treatment of OCD helps patients learn to tolerate this uncertainty.

Forced Behavior Change

It is heartbreaking to have to include this paragraph in a book about OCD treatment, but it is necessary. A person with OCD does not choose to have obsessive thoughts. In fact, they will tell you that they would be willing to do almost anything to make them stop. Behavior change requires that the behavior to be changed is voluntary. Involuntary behaviors cannot be voluntarily changed, not even by force. Is it possible to tell someone not to sneeze? Can you demand that they never urinate again? How about tell them to stop breathing? These sound like absurd examples, but it is the same as telling a person with OCD to just stop their obsessions and resulting compulsions.

In rare cases, some parents have been known, at worst, to tie their children down, and at best, punish them to stop them from performing cleaning compulsions. They may also verbally abuse them when they engage in OCD behaviors. These responses are borne from the parent's frustration, fear, and misunderstanding of OCD. Forced behavior change should never be used to respond to OCD. It is unmitigated torture and completely unacceptable, always.

Failure to Include Loved Ones

OCD patients can be embarrassed about their diagnosis. They may feel that their compulsions are putting a burden on their loved ones, and they may want to work on treatment by themselves. It is important to respect a patient's concerns and educate them about proper treatment protocol. For OCD, if a patient engages in exposure therapy during a session and then goes back home and their loved ones accommodate their OCD, then much, if not all, of the progress made in session will be erased. At the beginning of therapy, I explain the need to include loved ones in the treatment process. It is essential that they understand OCD and that, for treatment to be effective, they must stop accommodating their loved one.

I then teach them the Accommodon't [TM] process described in this book to give them the tools on how to stop accommodating.

Medication

Not every OCD patient needs medication. I always start working with patients very conservatively and use evidence-based therapy techniques before considering medication. Many patients benefit from therapy alone and never need medication. But some patients do benefit from medication to augment their therapy. Medication alone may help alleviate some OCD symptoms, but it does not resolve the underlying issue.

The biggest problem I see with medication relates back to providers who are not educated in OCD treatment. I always tell my patients to seek medication advice from a psychiatrist who is specially trained to treat OCD. This is because there are a lot of different medication options for OCD. The same medications are used to treat anxiety and depression, but the usual doses of those medications are very different, often much higher, for OCD. It is not uncommon for a new patient to report that "I tried medications, but they didn't help." When I ask about which medication they used and at what dose and, after receiving feedback from a psychiatrist trained in OCD, it turns out that the patient may have been on the correct medication but at a dose that is ineffective to treat OCD. Please note, I stress "psychiatrist" over a general practitioner because OCD is unique, and psychiatrists are specifically trained in treating mental health disorders.

Chapter Two
Other Related Disorders

ccurate diagnosis is an essential component of effective treatment. Correctly diagnosing OCD can be challenging because several other disorders involve ritualized, repetitive, or compulsive behavior, including obsessive-compulsive personality disorder (OCPD), autism spectrum disorder (ASD), hoarding, body dysmorphia, body-focused repetitive behaviors, and anxiety disorders. The key to differentiating OCD from these other disorders is understanding why the individual is engaging in repetitive or compulsive behavior.

OCD obsessions cause considerable distress because they do not align with the individual's values. They are intrusive thoughts or images that are disturbing, alarming, and not things that the individual wants to be thinking about. The level of distress becomes so significant and intolerable that the individual performs compulsions to reduce this distress. This is the hallmark of OCD: obsessions that cause clinically significant distress prompt individuals to engage in compulsions designed to reduce this distress. In other disorders that present with repetitive or compulsive behaviors, these behaviors are serving a purpose other than reducing the distress caused by obsessions.

Obsessive-Compulsive Personality Disorder (OCPD)

The DSM-V defines OCPD as "a pervasive pattern of preoccupation with orderliness, perfectionism, and mental and interpersonal control, at the expense of flexibility, openness, and efficiency (APA, 2013, p. 678). People with OCPD are often so preoccupied with the details, rules, and organization of a task that the objective of the task is lost. They may be unable to complete tasks because they never feel like it is done perfectly. Their devotion to work and productivity precludes participation in leisure activities or friendships. People with OCPD are often overly scrupulous and inflexible, making it difficult to interact positively with them, as no one meets their excessively high standards.

Many of the behaviors associated with OCPD can be mistaken for OCD. Perfectionism, scrupulosity, and compulsive behaviors like strictly following routines, excessive cleaning or organizing, or repeating tasks until completed perfectly, can make it difficult to differentiate between the two disorders. However, unlike OCD compulsions, these behaviors are not efforts to reduce the distress caused by obsessions, but rather follow from their rigid belief in doing things "the right way."

Another difference is the level of distress associated with the behaviors. Perhaps the easiest way to differentiate OCPD from OCD is that behaviors in OCPD are ego-syntonic while the same behavior in OCD is ego-dystonic.

Patients with OCD do not want to perform compulsions but feel powerless to stop them, which causes significant distress, while people with OCPD do not generally feel distressed by their behavior.

For example, a patient with OCPD may compulsively organize his pantry, spending hours lining up canned goods and organizing other food items. He is engaging in this behavior because, in his mind, this is the only "right" way to do it. His behavior aligns with his values, but goes too far, as evidenced by the amount of time devoted to the task and his inability to tolerate other views regarding pantry organization. This is very different from someone with OCD who obsessively organizes a pantry, ensuring that every item is in a specific place, to reduce the distress caused by an intrusive thought of harm befalling a loved one. While the behavior of obsessively organizing the pantry is the same, the reason why the behavior is performed is different.

Autism Spectrum Disorder (ASD)

ASD is a complex neurodevelopmental disorder that involves persistent difficulties in communication and social interactions, restrictive, repetitive patterns of behavior, interests, and activities, and sensory sensitivities or aversions. It can be challenging to differentiate between OCD and ASD because the repetitive behaviors and routines associated with ASD can look very similar to OCD compulsions. While these behaviors may look like OCD, they are not performed in response to an obsessive thought. For example, someone with ASD may insist on taking the same route to school every day or eating the same foods each day, but these behaviors are driven by a need for predictability and routine. Someone with OCD may feel compelled to take the same route each day or only eat specific foods, but these compulsions are driven by fear and anxiety caused by obsessions.

Once again, the key to distinguishing the compulsions of OCD from repetitive or ritualized behavior observed in ASD is understanding the reason for the behavior. If the repetitive or ritualized behavior occurs universally, regardless of situational factors, or is performed to preserve sameness/predictability, to increase, decrease, or modulate stimulation, to provide pleasure, or to communicate a desire or need, it is part of ASD, not OCD. If the behavior is present only in certain situations and the person does not want to engage in the behavior but feels powerless to stop it, then it is likely an OCD compulsion.

Hoarding

Hoarding disorder is characterized by "persistent difficulty discarding or parting with possessions, regardless of their actual value" (APA, 2013, p. 247). People with this disorder often accumulate items excessively, despite having no need or space for them. Hoarding often results from excessive sentimental attachment to items, fears of losing important items, or fears of not having something that is needed, rather than reflecting an attempt to neutralize distress caused by obsessions or intrusive thoughts. Unlike the compulsions of OCD, hoarding behavior is consistent with the individual's values in that people suffering from this disorder believe that they will need the items and experience considerable distress at the idea of getting rid of them.

Unlike OCD compulsions, hoarding does not cause distress in people with this disorder. While hoarding can escalate to the point that it significantly interferes with their ability to work, have relationships with others, or even maintain a safe environment, people with hoarding disorder genuinely desire to possess the hoarded items and are not typically distressed by their hoarding.

People with OCD may have hoarding compulsions, but this can be differentiated from hoarding disorder by examining the reason for the hoarding. Someone with contamination OCD may hoard items that they have touched to avoid contaminating others. Or someone with OCD may avoid throwing things away to avoid elaborate washing or checking rituals that discarding the objects would trigger. In these cases, hoarding behavior is a compulsion designed to reduce the distress associated with germ-related obsessions. Additionally, people with OCD involving hoarding compulsions are distressed by their behavior and would like to stop but feel powerless to do so.

Body Dysmorphia and Body-Focused Repetitive Behaviors (BFRBs)

Body dysmorphia involves a preoccupation with perceived imperfections or flaws in one's physical appearance and can involve repetitive behaviors like mirror checking, excessive grooming, and reassurance seeking that can look like OCD compulsions. However, body dysmorphia can be differentiated from OCD in that the focus of these behaviors is solely on physical appearance. Also, the behaviors reflect attempts to improve physical appearance, rather than to mitigate the distress caused by obsessions. Additionally, people with OCD generally have good insight into the irrationality of their compulsions but feel compelled to perform them to reduce the distress caused by obsessions. People with body dysmorphia frequently have poor insight and firmly believe that others find them "hideous" and engage in compulsive behavior to improve their appearance.

The DSM-V (APA, 2013) presents trichotillomania (hair-pulling disorder), excoriation (skin-picking) disorder, and body-focused repetitive behavior disorder (e.g., nail biting, lip biting, cheek chewing) as disorders related to OCD. As in the case of OCD compulsions, the repetitive behaviors that characterize these disorders do not align with the individual's values and cause clinically significant distress, including shame, embarrassment, and loss of control over behavior. However, unlike OCD compulsions, these behaviors are not attempts to reduce the distress caused by specific intrusive thoughts or obsessions. Rather, people with these disorders engage in these BFRBs for a variety of reasons, including relieving emotional states like boredom, satisfying a sensory need, or generating feelings of gratification or pleasure.

Generalized Anxiety Disorder

Generalized anxiety disorder (GAD) is another anxiety disorder that can be mistaken for OCD. It is a chronic and excessive state of worry and anxiety that extends beyond specific triggers or situations. Individuals with GAD often experience persistent, widespread, and uncontrollable feelings of apprehension, fear, and nervousness, even when there is no apparent reason for concern. The worries in GAD typically involve various aspects of everyday life, such as health, work, finances, family, and relationships. These anxious thoughts can be all-encompassing and interfere significantly with daily functioning, leading to difficulty in concentrating, restlessness, irritability, muscle tension, and sleep disturbances.

GAD affects both the emotional and physical well-being of those who experience it, and it often leads to a sense of chronic unease and heightened sensitivity to potential threats, making it challenging to relax and enjoy life fully. Management of GAD often involves a combination of cognitive-behavioral therapy, medication, and relaxation techniques to help individuals regain a sense of control over their worries and lead a more balanced and fulfilling life.

Other Anxiety Disorders

Anxiety disorders are characterized by excessive fear and anxiety, which leads to dysfunctional behavior, most notably, avoidance. The fear and anxiety of these disorders can be difficult to distinguish from OCD obsessions, while the avoidance and safety behaviors can look like compulsions. Correctly differentiating between OCD and other anxiety disorders requires a clear understanding of the purpose of excessive worry and avoidance. Evaluating the relationship between distressing thoughts and the individual's values can provide further diagnostic clues.

Several anxiety disorders cause people to completely avoid situations that trigger their anxiety or fear. For example, people with a specific phobia of heights will go out of their way to avoid high places, people with social anxiety disorder will do almost anything to avoid public speaking or other social situations, people with panic disorder will avoid activities that may trigger panic attacks, and the avoidance of people with agoraphobia can escalate to the point of becoming housebound. Rather than attempting to minimize the distress caused by their fears by engaging in compulsions, people with anxiety disorders go to extreme lengths to avoid their triggers completely, which significantly interferes with working, going to school, and maintaining relationships.

Chapter Three

OCD Treatment

OCD is a chronic mental health condition that is characterized by recurring, unwanted thoughts (obsessions) and repetitive behaviors or mental acts (compulsions). While there is currently no known cure for OCD, it can be effectively managed and treated. Treatment for OCD typically involves a combination of therapy, medication, and self-help strategies. The main therapy used for OCD is exposure and response prevention (ERP). ERP involves gradually exposing patients to their obsessions and preventing the corresponding compulsive behaviors. Medications such as selective serotonin reuptake inhibitors (SSRIs) are often prescribed to help manage the symptoms of OCD. These medications can help regulate the brain's serotonin levels, which are believed to play a role in OCD.

It's important to note that treatment outcomes can vary from person to person. Some patients may experience significant symptom reduction or remission with treatment, while others may experience more ongoing symptoms. However, with appropriate treatment and support, many people with OCD can lead fulfilling lives and effectively manage their symptoms. Regular therapy sessions, medication management, and implementing self-care strategies are essential in maintaining symptom control and minimizing the impact of OCD on daily functioning.

DRIL

DRIL uses core concepts of Inference-Based Cognitive Behavioral Therapy (I-CBT) developed by Kieron O'Connor and Frederick Aardema and explained in their book "The Inference-Based approach to obsessive-compulsive disorder: a Clinician's Handbook for Obsessive Compulsive Disorder" (O'Connor, & Aardema, 2012) and Exposure and Response Prevention (ERP) therapy originally created by Stanley Robinson in the 1970's and expertly explained by Edna B. Foa, Elna Yadin, and Tracey K. Lichner in their book "Treating Your OCD with Exposure and Response (Ritual) Prevention" (Foa, Yadin, & Lichner, 2012). In the subsequent section of this book, I will walk you through how I use DRIL to develop an individualized treatment plan for my patients.

Evaluation

Pre-Treatment Foundational Analysis

In my practice, I use the first session with new patients as an opportunity to learn everything I can about them and their background. I am especially interested in their possible OCD, but I can only develop an accurate diagnosis when I am able to understand their symptoms in context, including any possible co-occurring disorders. For purposes of this book, I will explain the main information that I believe is important for a therapist to gather to facilitate making an accurate diagnosis. This explanation is not fully comprehensive as a competent therapist will be capable of analyzing the patient's answers and asking appropriate follow-ups. This information is illustrative only.

1. Relationships. I want to know about the people in the patient's life. This includes parents, partners, siblings, children, friends, and close relatives. I want to know how they perceive these relationships and whether they are stressful or supportive. My goal is to understand the patient's support system.

2. Housing. Where does the patient live, who do they live with and what is the environment like? A patient living by themselves in a small apartment in a crowded community will have different experiences from someone living in a spacious home in the suburbs. Do they live with others? How do they interact with them? Is anyone in the home accommodating their OCD? Are they in a hostile environment?

3. Employment. Is the patient employed? What type of work do they do? Do they work from home, or do they have coworkers whom they regularly see? Is the environment calm or stressful? Do they experience OCD at work? Do any coworkers accommodate them?

4. Education. What is their educational background? How do they think? Are they a verbal or visual learner, etc.? What subject matter interests them?

This information will help me introduce concepts in a way that the patient can understand.

5. Stressors. Is the patient experiencing any current significant life stressors? Money, health, work, relationships, deaths, moves, etc. Stress often can lead to OCD flare-ups. It may be hard to focus on therapy if there is something else distracting them.

6. Obsessions. I want to understand historical obsessive thoughts as well as any current obsessions. What is the thought? How does it make them feel? How do they react to it? Do they experience any physical sensations? This information allows me to start thinking about possible exposures. It is also important to explore what the patient believes might happen because of their thought? Is it distressing to think about relieving themself of the thought? This could be a block to effective therapy.

7. Compulsions. What does the patient do when they have an obsessive thought? It is important to understand these responses in detail. It also allows me to think about what I need to avoid during treatment so that I stay away from reinforcing compulsions.

8. Severity. How much time does the patient spend engaged in obsessions and compulsions? Is it consecutive, time or is it intermittent throughout the day?

9. Onset. I will ask the patient to describe what was happening in their life at the time that the obsessions started. Sometimes they will report that they have had obsessions since childhood. Sometimes they will describe a specific traumatic event that seemed to have occurred before they noticed their OCD.

10. Family history of OCD. It is common that someone with OCD will report that a parent, grandparent, or close relative has or had OCD. It helps to know this when gathering the big picture for purposes of diagnosing their condition.

11. Physical health. Does the patient have any physical health problems? Have they visited a medical doctor recently? Are they receiving any treatments for any conditions?

12. Mental health. What is the patient's mental health history? Have they been diagnosed with any mental health condition? Are they currently seeing another therapist or have they seen anyone in the past? Why did they seek therapy? What treatments did they receive? Was the therapy effective?

13. Medication. Is the patient taking any medications for any physical conditions? Mental conditions? What are the details? What are they taking and what doses? When did they start/stop taking it? How did they respond? Who prescribed it?

14. OCD Treatments. If not already disclosed, has the patient sought OCD treatment already? Who diagnosed them? What treatment did they receive? How did they respond?

Y-BOCS

The Yale-Brown Obsessive-Compulsive Scale (Y-BOCS) is a widely used and well-established assessment tool designed to measure the severity of symptoms in individuals with OCD. It was developed by Wayne K. Goodman and his colleagues at Yale University in the 1980s.

The Y-BOCS consists of two parts: the Symptom Checklist and the Severity Scale. Here's a breakdown of each component:

1. Symptom Checklist: The Symptom Checklist is a comprehensive list of common obsessions and compulsions experienced by individuals with OCD. It covers various symptom categories such as contamination, hoarding, symmetry, aggressive thoughts, and sexual thoughts. The individual reports whether each listed obsession and compulsion are present now, in the past only, or never occurred.

2. Severity Scale: The Severity Scale assesses the overall severity of OCD symptoms. It includes ratings for the time spent on obsessions and compulsions, interference with daily functioning, distress caused by the symptoms, resistance to thoughts and rituals, and control over the symptoms.

Each item is rated on a scale from 0 (no symptoms) to 4 (extreme symptoms).

The Y-BOCS provides a structured and standardized way to assess the severity of OCD symptoms. It helps clinicians determine the impact of OCD on an individual's life, track changes in symptom severity over time, and assess treatment outcomes. It is often administered through an interview format by a qualified mental health professional who is familiar with the scale. When I first started administering the Y-BOCS, I would provide it to the patient for them to complete prior to the first session. My experiences with this method taught me that the Y-BOCS should be administered in session by the clinician. The reason is that patients often have questions for clarification, and it is easier for the clinician to follow up on specific issues while the patient is thinking about them.

It's important to note that the Y-BOCS is not intended to be a standalone diagnostic tool but rather a clinical aid to assess symptom severity and track progress. It can be re-administered during the treatment process to track progress.

Functional tracking (self-monitoring form)

Once the clinician completes the Foundational Analysis and the Y-BOCS, it is helpful to have the patient complete a self-monitoring form. I use a form based on the work of Yadin, Foa, & Lichner. The patient will note the time of day that they had an obsessive thought. They will briefly describe the situation, activity, or obsessive thought they had. Next, they will rate its severity using a Subjective Units of Distress Score (SUDS) of zero to 100 where zero is no distress at all and 100 is the most distress they can imagine. Then, they will describe the compulsion or ritual in which they engaged to reduce their distress. Finally, they will note how long the entire situation took.

This monitoring form accomplishes several tasks. First, it helps to clarify for the clinician the current obsessions and compulsions. Second, it establishes whether there is a pattern associated with their thoughts. Third, it forces the patient to actively notice their obsessions and resulting compulsions.

Several of my patients have reported that this exercise alone, before we even began treatment in earnest, had a therapeutic effect that helped them to gain a clear understanding of their OCD. As a result, treatment was easier for them because they understood their actions and knew how they wanted to focus.

OCD SELF-MONITORING FORM: Date: _______________				
Time	Situation/ Thought	SUDS (0-100)	Describe Ritual	Minutes Spent
12:00 - 1:00 AM				
1:00 - 2:00 AM				
2:00 - 3:00 AM				
3:00 - 4:00 AM				
4:00 - 5:00 AM				
5:00 - 6:00 AM				
6:00 - 7:00 AM				
7:00 - 8:00 AM				

8:00 - 9:00 AM				
9:00 - 10:00 AM				
10:00 - 11:00 AM				
11:00 - 12:00 PM				
12:00 - 1:00 PM				
1:00 - 2:00 PM				
2:00 - 3:00 PM				
3:00 - 4:00 PM				
4:00 - 5:00 PM				
5:00 - 6:00 PM				
6:00 - 7:00 PM				
7:00 - 8:00 PM				
8:00 - 9:00 PM				
9:00 - 10:00 PM				
10:00 - 11:00 PM				
11:00 - 12:00 AM				

Appendix

Doubt-Reduction Psychoeducation

The next stage of treatment is doubt-reduction psychoeducation based upon I-CBT teachings. I start by providing a graphic of the OCD thought process. When we are in the here and now, something (overt or covert) may happen that triggers a thought. Perhaps we have the thought that our hands are dirty.

OCD Cycle Graphic

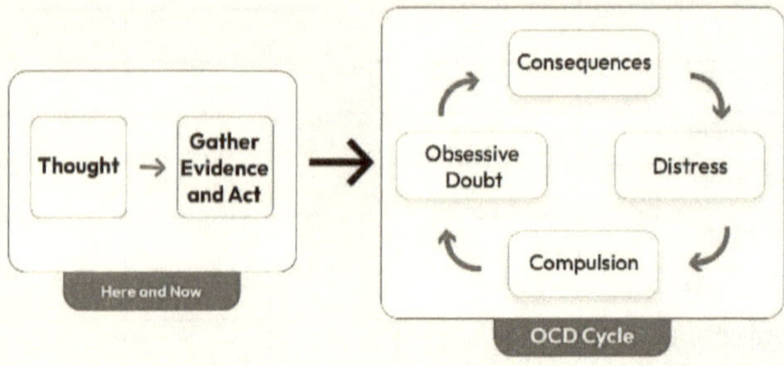

Evidence-Based

- See
- Hear
- Smell
- Touch
- Taste
- Known Facts

Doubt-Based

- Things out of your control
- Emotions over logic
- Confirmation bias
- Overgeneralization
- Complex over simple thinking
- Possibility becomes probability
- Anecdotes
- Hearsay
- False Causation

I explain that in OCD, we start by operating in the here and now and eventually cross over into the OCD cycle. In the here and now we are dealing with identifiable facts. This means using what we know as well as what we can sense with our five senses taste, touch, hear, see, smell). For example, if I have the thought that my hands are dirty, I have the benefit of knowing where they have been, and I have the benefit of my senses. So, if I believe my hands are dirty and I know that I just picked up a load of dirty trash with my bare hands that the raccoons took out of my trashcan, then I know that I have touched dirt. I can also see dirt and slime on my hands, feel grease and grime and smell bad odors. The here and now tells me my hands are objectively dirty and need to be washed.

But what about OCD? Consider that I have the thought that my hands might be dirty. I then evaluate what I know. I just came out of the shower where I washed my whole body. I have not touched anything dirty since leaving the shower. I do not see any dirt on my hands, they do not feel dirty, and they even smell fresh from soap. Therefore, my hands are not dirty. That should be the end of the thought and I would move on with my day. Not so for OCD.

In OCD, I get pulled into the CD cycle. This starts with obsessive doubt. Doubt is defined as knowing the facts but just not believing them. OCD is an expert at causing us to doubt the facts. In fact, this is what OCD lives for! So, OCD now steps in with its tools, the doubt lexicon. It makes us question what we know to be true, and it does this with a lexicon that makes achieving certainty or clarity impossible. For example, OCD may cause us to question our senses. "It's possible that your hands really are dirty, but you just can't see the dirt." "You used a paper towel to dry your hands after you washed them, and I heard that paper towels are white because they go through a bleaching process during manufacture. Bleach is harmful, so your hands must be contaminated!"

OCD effectively used the doubt lexicon in those statements. It used probability over possibility, overgeneralization, complex over simple thinking, and hearsay. As you can see, OCD is adept at its game. And it knows that you can neither prove nor disprove any of what it says, unless you recognize that you are using the OCD doubt lexicon and move out of the OCD cycle and into the here and now. When looking at the situation objectively in the here and now, you know that your hands are probably clean and there is no reasonable fear.

I realize that you most likely picked up on my last statement "…you know that your hands are *probably* clean." I said *probably* because there are no guarantees in life, and I don't want to engage in a false narrative. I'm sure that we can all come up with a one-off situation where your hands may not be clean. But that would be a possibility, not a probability, whereas OCD wants you to believe that it is probable, not just possible.

At this point, I will work with patients to be sure they understand the OCD cycle and the doubt lexicon. I then ask them to track their obsessive thoughts over the next week, and throughout the remainder of treatment, by using the Obsessive Doubt tracking chart.

Obsessive Doubt Tracking

1) Things beyond your control, 2) Emotion over logic, 3) Confirmation bias, 4) Complex over simple thinking,
5) Possibility becomes probability, 6) Overgeneralization, 7) Anecdotes, 8) Hearsay, 9) False causation

What is the Obsessive Thought?	Facts/ Senses Proof (See, smell, touch, taste, hear)	Who are you according to your core values?	What is the Obsessive Doubt	Obsessive doubts proof to support it
My hands may be contaminated and I could spread it and that could make me sick.	I went to the store and bought groceries. I do not see any dirt on my hands, I do not feel anything sticky, I do not smell anything on my hands.	I value being a clean person with good personal hygiene.	I have no evidence of any dirt on my hands but I just can't believe it. I went out and touched things so I must be contaminated.	2, 5

Appendix

The purpose of this exercise is to identify and highlight when they are operating in the here and now versus when they move over into the OCD cycle.

Exposure and Response Prevention

Once the patient understands the OCD cycle and the doubt lexicon, the next step in treatment is Exposure and Response Prevention (ERP). ERP is a specific form of cognitive-behavioral therapy (CBT) widely used in the treatment of OCD. It is based on the idea that exposure to obsessive thoughts and the subsequent prevention of compulsive behaviors can help individuals break free from the cycle of distress and compulsion. The goal is to achieve inhibitory learning so that the patient is equipped to deal with obsessive doubts that are occurring now or that may occur in the future.

Overview of ERP

1. Psychoeducation: The therapist educates the patient about the principles of ERP therapy, explaining that the purpose is for the patient to achieve inhibitory learning by gradually facing their obsessive doubt and eliminating their need to engage in compulsive behaviors.

2. Building an exposure hierarchy: The patient and therapist work together to create a list, known as an exposure hierarchy, which ranks situations or stimuli related to the obsessions from least distressing to most distressing.

3. Exposure: The patient is exposed to the situations or triggers that evoke obsessive thoughts and distress, starting with an item on the hierarchy that rates approximately 50 on a subjective units of distress (SUDS) scale. This is a number from 0 to 100 rating the intensity of the patient's distress. Exposure can be conducted in real life (*in vivo* exposure) or imagined by the patient (imaginal exposure). Additionally, advanced exposure opportunities using virtual reality, real 360° images, augmented reality, and more are becoming available. A good resource for therapists is www.rxxrt.com. This site allows therapists to inexpensively provide 360° exposures to their patients either online or in the office. The therapist may also include interoceptive elements with the exposure. Interoceptive elements are designed to trigger somatic feelings (i.e., increased heart rate, hyperventilation, dizziness) along with the exposure. If a patient reports that heights make them feel dizziness along with their distress, the therapist may spin the patient in place several times to trigger a dizzy feeling before beginning therapy.

4. Response prevention (also known as ritual prevention): During exposure, the patient is instructed to resist the urge to engage in the usual compulsive behaviors or rituals that they typically perform to reduce distress. This is known as response prevention. By preventing the usual response, the

patient works with the therapist to achieve inhibitory learning. In general, the patient learns to manage their distress and realizes that it will naturally diminish over time without the need for compulsions.

5. Gradual progression: The exposure and response prevention exercises are repeated over multiple sessions, gradually moving up the hierarchy to more challenging situations. As inhibitory learning increases, the patient's obsessive doubt becomes less powerful, and they learn to tolerate anxiety without the need for compulsive behaviors.

6. Maintenance and relapse prevention: After completing the initial phase of ERP therapy, patients are encouraged to continue practicing the skills they have learned to maintain their progress. They may also develop relapse prevention strategies to identify early warning signs and implement coping techniques if symptoms resurface.

ERP therapy can be intense and, when performed correctly, will initially evoke anxiety and distress. However, with the guidance and support of a qualified therapist, patients gradually learn to tolerate the anxiety triggered by their obsessions without resorting to compulsions. Over time, this process can lead to a reduction in the frequency and intensity of obsessions and compulsions, allowing individuals to regain control over their lives.

Building an Exposure Hierarchy

At this point, the OCD obsessions and compulsions are well-defined. A separate hierarchy is developed for each compulsion. The therapist works with the patient to develop a tiered list of exposure events that will trigger the patient's anxiety and rates the reported SUDS score of each event.

It is important that the therapist and patient develop a hierarchy of realistic exposures. The therapist must consider whether the exposures can be conducted in-office or are better accomplished through Telehealth. Some exposures are best done in-person somewhere around town and the therapist must consider whether such exposures are feasible.

Once the hierarchy is created, each exposure option is equated with a numerical SUDS score between 0 and 100 and ranked. A sample hierarchy for a patient with contamination obsessions related to doorknobs could look like this:

Exposure	SUDS
Look at a photograph of a doorknob	10
Touch a doorknob in my house	20
Look at a photograph of a dirty doorknob	30
Touch a doorknob in public	50
Touch and hold a doorknob in public	60
Touch a doorknob in public then come home and touch my bed pillow without first washing my hands	80
Touch a doorknob in public then touch my face	90
Touch a doorknob in public then eat a sandwich without washing my hands	100

Inhibitory Learning

Inhibitory learning is the process through which a patient learns to respond to obsessive doubt in a realistic and healthy manner. Ultimately, the patient will replace inappropriate or maladaptive responses to obsessive doubt (i.e. compulsions) with new learning, like the realization that their anxiety and distress will eventually diminish, and that there is no need to perform short-lived compulsions. It involves acquiring new information that contradicts the original fear or anxiety associated with a specific stimulus or situation. With repeated exposure, the patient learns that the feared consequences of their obsessions do not occur. Inhibitory learning sets the stage for patients to experience habituation, disconfirmation of OCD beliefs, increased tolerance of distress and uncertainty. These experiences build a sense of mastery and self-efficacy, which further strengthen patients' motivation for and confidence in their ability to recover from OCD.

New Learning

New learning is acquired using doubt reduction techniques. In doubt reduction, the patient learns to identify when their thoughts are tied to the here and now with facts, data, and proof. They also become well versed in the doubt lexicon, so they are able to identify when they have entered the OCD cycle. By tracking their obsessive doubt and then identifying whether it is borne from facts or the doubt lexicon, they can strengthen their awareness of when they are in control of their thoughts versus when OCD is controlling their thoughts.

Habituation

Habituation refers to the process by which individuals with OCD experience a decrease in the intensity and distress associated with their obsessions over time. It is a natural psychological phenomenon that occurs when a person is repeatedly exposed to a specific trigger or situation, leading to a reduced emotional response. Habituation occurs due to a process called extinction, which involves the weakening of the conditioned response (anxiety and distress) that is associated with the conditioned stimulus (the trigger or obsession). When individuals repeatedly confront the trigger without engaging in compulsive behavior, their fear response gradually decreases. The brain learns that the trigger is not actually dangerous or threatening, leading to a reduction in the emotional response associated with it. Additionally, habituation helps patients recognize that distress and anxiety will dissipate over time and that these feelings are unavoidable, manageable, and not inherently dangerous.

Disconfirmation

Disconfirmation addresses a patient's deeply ingrained beliefs about the perceived threat or danger linked to their obsessions. These beliefs can be irrational, exaggerated, and not supported by evidence or logic. Disconfirmation provides evidence that contradicts these distorted beliefs and challenges the individual's negative expectations. By actively engaging in exposures without performing a compulsive response, patients have an opportunity to learn that their feared outcomes do not come true and that the anticipated negative consequences do not occur. This disconfirms their original beliefs and expectations, providing evidence that challenges the accuracy and validity of their obsessions.

As patients repeatedly face their fears and find that the feared negative consequences do not occur, the disconfirmation process strengthens. Over time, the patient's automatic association between the trigger and the compulsion weakens, as the irrational beliefs associated with their obsessions are gradually replaced by more adaptive and realistic ones.

It is important to note that disconfirmation is not about disproving every worry or fear a patient may have. OCD beliefs do respond to logic or reason. That is why talk therapy does not work for OCD. Instead, OCD beliefs respond to experiences through the inhibitory learning processes described above. This shift in thinking is created by repeated demonstrations that the feared outcomes are unlikely or unsupported by evidence. This process helps patients gain a more balanced and realistic perspective, reducing the power and influence of obsessions on their daily lives.

Increased Tolerance

Increased tolerance refers to the process of helping patients with OCD develop a greater ability to cope with and accept uncertainty in their lives. Patients with OCD often experience an intense fear of uncertain outcomes and a heightened need for certainty. In OCD treatment, increasing tolerance to uncertainty involves challenging and modifying the patient's beliefs about the need for certainty and the negative consequences associated with uncertainty. The goal is to help patients recognize that uncertainty is a normal and unavoidable part of life and that seeking absolute certainty is neither realistic nor necessary.

During the treatment process, patients are encouraged to examine and challenge their beliefs about uncertainty. They learn to identify and question their irrational thoughts and catastrophic interpretations of uncertain situations. As they engage in ERP and actively confront uncertainty, they begin to experience a reduction in anxiety and distress over time.

Increasing tolerance to uncertainty is a gradual and ongoing process in OCD treatment. Over time, patients develop new coping strategies and adaptive responses to uncertainty, which can be generalized to other areas of their lives. They become less reliant on compulsions as a means of managing uncertainty and are better equipped to handle the uncertainties and ambiguities that arise in everyday situations. It empowers them to face uncertainties with greater resilience, flexibility, and acceptance, ultimately promoting long-term recovery and well-being.

Mastery

Patients with OCD often feel overwhelmed and controlled by their intrusive thoughts and the urge to engage in compulsive behaviors. Through the process of mastery, patients experience a shift in their beliefs about their ability to control and manage their OCD symptoms. As they successfully confront their fears and resist compulsions, they develop a greater sense of self-efficacy and mastery over their condition. This newfound confidence translates into improved daily functioning and a reduced impact of OCD on their lives. Achieving mastery does not mean the complete elimination of OCD symptoms. Rather, it involves developing the skills and resilience to effectively cope with and manage symptoms when they arise. Mastery serves as a foundation for long-term recovery, allowing patients to maintain progress and successfully navigate future challenges related to their OCD.

Post-Exposure Processing

After each exposure session, the therapist reviews the inhibitory learning concepts with the patient and evaluates the patient's achievements. It is important that both therapist and patient remain aware of their goals and continually monitor progress. In OCD, progress can occur quickly for some patients and more slowly for others. By conducting post-exposure processing, the therapist can more readily identify both progress and opportunities to modify future exposures to best achieve inhibitory learning.

Relapse Prevention

The final step in the OCD treatment process is relapse prevention. There are four distinct topics to cover with every patient when discussing the final stages of their treatment.

1. Reflect on progress.

It is important to reflect on the progress patients have made. When they first come to therapy, patients are typically overwhelmed with distress from uncontrolled obsessive doubt. They may be engaging in compulsions that significantly restrict their ability to function and sometimes they may even be homebound. Highlighting the patient's achievements and praising them for having the courage to engage in exposure therapy can go a long way toward building their long-term confidence.

2. Reflect on useful strategies.

Take time to review all the new learning so that the patient can keep all of their new knowledge in perspective. Remember, they have done a lot of learning and practical application. Now is the time to summarize for them. It is helpful to review the OCD cycle with them and remind them to be conscious of when they are in the here and now as well as when they are crossing over into the OCD cycle. A review of the doubt lexicon is important at this point so that they keep it fresh in their mind and understand that when they are using that lexicon it means they are entering the world of obsessive doubt.

It is also important to review the elements of inhibitory learning. Repeating the elements of new learning, habituation, disconfirmation, increased tolerance, and mastery will help them appreciate the amount of work they have done to prepare themselves for any future bouts with OCD.

3. Plan for tackling remaining issues.

Be sure to help them plan a healthy path forward. This means that they need to continue encouraging loved ones to refrain from accommodating any future obsessive doubts and engage in the Accommodon't[TM] process when necessary. Because OCD is something that will always be a part of their life, patients should be forewarned not to drop their guard. If they are taking medication, then they should remain on the medication and follow their doctor's orders.

Patients can also continue practicing awareness of the obsessive doubt lexicon by using the tracking form that they used in treatment. Now is not the time to ease up on progress. Emphasize that the new neural pathways that have been built during therapy need to be strengthened and that this requires them to continue reinforcing all the good habits that they have learned. Continued awareness of the OCD cycle and practicing the healthy skills they have learned will solidify their actions as a new way of life.

4. Plan for relapse

Relapse is a real possibility because OCD is not ever considered to be cured. The goal is that the patient has learned more about how OCD works *and* how they can address it and keep it at bay. But just like they have learned that there are no guarantees in life, they must accept that OCD may come back and challenge them in the future. At this point, it is important that they have predetermined which actions they will take to avoid relapse. Each patient will develop their own plan. Effective plans will probably include the names and telephone numbers of loved ones who understand what the patient has gone through and can be supportive during a relapse episode. Additionally, the patient should not feel as if they need to tackle relapse alone and should be instructed to contact their treatment provider at the earliest signs of relapse. Also, be sure to include any specific strategies that the patient believes would be effective for them.

Challenges to ERP

While exposure and response prevention (ERP) therapy is an effective treatment for OCD, it's administration can present several challenges. Some of the difficulties encountered during ERP therapy include:

1. Initial resistance: Many individuals with OCD may initially resist engaging in exposure exercises due to the distress and anxiety associated with confronting their fears. The idea of intentionally provoking anxiety can be intimidating, leading to reluctance or avoidance.

2. Identifying exposures: The form that OCD obsessions can take is unlimited. Successful ERP depends on the therapist and patient working closely together to identify specific obsessive thoughts. This is crucial for creating exposure hierarchies and designing exposures. Only the patient knows what will cause them distress. In some cases, it is difficult to identify exposures for therapy because the exposures need to be accomplished in the office during a 50-minute session. The therapist cannot easily leave their office to meet a patient in a specific location, such as numerous public restrooms. If the obsession involves something inside of an airplane, the therapist cannot realistically book a flight with the patient. Or the obsession may relate to wild animals or thoughts about jumping off a ski lift;

situations that are not easy to access. Extended reality is gaining in popularity and making these exposures more accessible. Prescription XRT (www.rxxrt.com) is designed to provide inexpensive access to realistic exposure experiences so that therapists may conduct ERP either in-office or remotely.

3. Anxiety escalation: During exposure, anxiety levels may initially increase before gradually decreasing over time. This initial spike in anxiety can be distressing for individuals and may deter them from continuing with the therapy.

4. High levels of distress: Exposure exercises can induce significant distress, as individuals are intentionally exposing themselves to their feared situations or triggers. This heightened distress can make it challenging for individuals to tolerate the exposure and complete the therapy sessions.

5. Avoidance behaviors: Individuals with OCD often engage in avoidance behaviors to alleviate anxiety. These behaviors can act as barriers to effective ERP as they prevent individuals from fully engaging in the exposure exercises necessary for habituation and disconfirmation of their fears.

6. Relapse and maintenance: After completing ERP therapy successfully, individuals may experience relapses or difficulties maintaining the gains

achieved. This highlights the importance of incorporating relapse prevention strategies and ongoing support to ensure long-term treatment success.

7. Treatment adherence: ERP therapy requires consistent effort, commitment, and adherence to treatment protocols. Adhering to the therapy regimen, which often includes regular exposure exercises and avoiding the associated compulsive behaviors, can be challenging for some individuals.

8. Treatment availability and access: Access to qualified ERP therapists and specialized OCD treatment centers may be limited in certain regions, making it difficult for individuals to access the therapy. This can result in delays or inadequate access to effective treatment. Luckily, many exposure therapists are offering their services through Telehealth.

9. Co-occurring conditions: OCD commonly co-occurs with other mental health conditions such as anxiety disorders or depression. Addressing and managing these comorbid conditions alongside OCD during ERP therapy can present additional challenges.

10. Therapist expertise: Effective implementation of ERP therapy requires therapists with expertise in OCD and experience in conducting exposure exercises. Finding a qualified therapist with the

necessary skills and experience can be challenging in some areas.

Despite these challenges, ERP therapy remains a highly recommended and evidence-based treatment for OCD. With appropriate support, guidance, and persistence, individuals can overcome these obstacles and experience significant improvement in their symptoms and overall quality of life.

Chapter Four

Virtual Reality Exposure Therapy

Virtual reality exposure therapy (VRET) operates from the same theoretical framework as *in vivo* (real life) and imaginal exposure therapy. However, unlike *in vivo* and imaginal exposures, VRET uses virtual reality (VR) to create virtual exposure environments that are tailored to each patient's specific needs. As in more traditional forms of exposure therapy, VRET is most effective when implemented as one component of a broader cognitive-behavioral treatment. Similarly, the effectiveness of VRET is enhanced when patients and therapists have a good working relationship, when the therapist provides psychoeducation to patients regarding the nature of anxiety and how it is maintained, and when the therapist helps patients develop cognitive strategies for identifying, testing, and replacing negative or false beliefs that help maintain anxiety and fear.

The ease with which VR technology can be used to create tailored virtual exposures for a broad range of patients is what sets VRET apart from other modalities of exposure therapy. Patients with specific phobias like fears of flying or snakes can face their fears in realistic, multi-sensory virtual environments. The same VR platform can be used to create virtual public speaking events for patients with social anxiety, or crowded subway cars for patients with panic disorder or agoraphobia. Additionally, VRET increases access to evidence-based therapy by enabling patients who live in remote areas, or in areas with few/no providers trained in exposure therapy, the opportunity to fully engage in effective treatment.

VRET may be particularly helpful for patients with OCD, as virtual exposures can be designed to target the broad spectrum of specific obsessions and compulsions characterizing OCD in a way that is impractical or impossible with more traditional *in vivo* exposure therapy. For example, a therapist and patient may spend considerable time planning and traveling to a restaurant to conduct an exposure session, only to find that the restaurant does not trigger the patient's specific obsessions and compulsions. With VRET the possibilities for exposures are nearly limitless; the therapist and patient can sift through various exposure environments within a single session to select one that effectively elicits the patient's OCD symptoms.

Virtual Reality Exposure Therapy for Anxiety Disorders

Being able to confidently embrace virtual exposures as a viable alternative to *in vivo* and imaginal exposures requires evidence that virtual environments can produce the anxiety and fear responses necessary for effective exposure therapy, that virtual exposures are at least as effective as *in vivo* exposures, and that treatment gains from VRET generalize to behavior changes in real life. The results of numerous studies investigating the efficacy of VRET for anxiety disorders support the efficacy of virtual exposures by showing that virtual exposures effectively elicit anxiety and fear and result in durable and meaningful changes in patients' lives. Reviews of several studies are presented below to highlight that VRET is effective across anxiety disorders and that the resulting decreases in anxiety/distress are consistent across assessment methods, including self-report, diagnostic interviews, and behavioral tasks.

There is substantial evidence that VRET is effective for treating specific phobias. Meyerbroker and colleagues (2022) found that VRET effectively reduced fears of flying and increased patients' self-efficacy. Similarly, Cote and Bouchard (2009) found that five sessions of 60-minute VRET for arachnophobia reduced anxiety, increased self-efficacy, and decreased avoidance, as indicated by self-report and performance on a behavioral avoidance test. Two large meta-analyses generated large effect sizes for VRET's ability to reduce phobic fears and demonstrated that VRET was at least as effective as traditional *in vivo* exposure therapy.

VR can be used to induce physiological symptoms for people with panic disorder and to create tailored VR environments for people with agoraphobia. VRET may be particularly useful for people with agoraphobia whose distress and anxiety can escalate to such a degree that they become unable to leave their homes. In a study comparing the effectiveness of VRET and *in vivo* exposure therapy for patients with panic disorder and agoraphobia, Quero et al. (2014) found that the treatments were similarly effective and that VRET was perceived as less aversive than *in vivo* exposure therapy. Two meta-analyses of VRET for agoraphobia reported similar effect sizes for VRET and *in vivo* exposure therapy (Meyerbroker & Emmelkamp, 2010; Weschler et al., 2019). Importantly, Meyerbroker and Emmelkamp found no significant differences between VRET and *in vivo* exposure therapy at a 3-month follow-up and reported that treatment gains using a virtual environment generalized to real-world behavior. A meta-analysis of VRET for panic disorder found a large effect size for VRET and noted that VRET was as effective as *in vivo* exposure therapy.

Initial concerns regarding whether interactions with virtual strangers could elicit anxiety in people with social anxiety disorder were dispelled by a study conducted by Morina and colleagues (2015). These researchers created a

VR program that included a wide variety of verbal interactions between patients and virtual humans; patients with social anxiety reported that the interactions with virtual humans triggered a similar level of social anxiety as social interactions in the real world. Anderson and colleagues (2005) compared VRET and group exposure therapy for social anxiety disorder and found that both treatments were effective, as demonstrated by self-ratings, a diagnostic interview, and performance on a behavioral speech task. Additionally, both treatments produced long-lasting benefits; treatment gains were maintained at a 4- to 6-year follow-up. In a randomized clinical trial (RCT) comparing CBT, CBT plus VRET, and a waitlist control group, Wallach and colleagues (2009) found CBT and CBT plus VRET to be similarly effective; however, twice as many patients dropped out of the CBT group, indicating that virtual exposures may be a preferable treatment option for patients with social anxiety. Moreover, in a meta-analysis comparing the effectiveness of VRET and *in vivo* exposure therapy for treating public speaking anxiety, both interventions were similarly effective (Reeves et al., 2022).

Although considerable research has shown that VRET is effective for treating specific anxiety disorders, it can be difficult to make broad conclusions based on results from studies with varying designs and different participants. Meta-analysis allows for comparison across studies and generates effect sizes to characterize the impact of interventions across large participant samples. Several meta-analyses comparing the efficacy of VRET to *in vivo* exposure therapy have shown that VRET is at least as effective as *in vivo* exposure therapy (Opris et al., 2012; Carl et al., 2019), with one meta-analysis revealing an advantage for VRET over *in vivo* exposure therapy (Powers & Emmelkamp, 2008). These meta-analyses also indicated that treatment gains achieved via VRET are durable and generalizable to real-world behavior and that VRET was consistently associated with increases in patients' self-efficacy.

Virtual Reality Exposure Therapy for OCD

Exposure and response prevention (ERP) is widely accepted as the evidence-based treatment for OCD. ERP requires the patient to intentionally expose themselves to objects, situations, or thoughts that trigger their obsessions, while refraining from compulsions, safety behaviors, or other strategies to reduce distress. OCD symptom reduction is achieved through the different types of learning that occur during ERP. Prior to engaging in ERP, specific objects, situations, or thoughts are imbued with fear and trigger obsessions in people with OCD. ERP allows patients to test these fear-based cognitions, or OCD beliefs, and sets the stage for inhibitory learning to occur when patients realize that the things that OCD says will happen do not happen or are extremely unlikely to happen. These fear-based cognitions, like an intrusive thought that touching a doorknob with bare fingers means that you will contaminate a loved one with a deadly virus, are not eliminated by ERP. The original fear-based thought remains in memory, but ERP enables patients to form new safety-based, or inhibitory, meanings for these objects/situations/thoughts. Successful ERP facilitates inhibitory learning by providing the opportunity to disconfirm OCD beliefs and increasing the patient's ability to access the non-threatening, inhibitory beliefs more easily and frequently, across various contexts and over time.

As patients engage in ERP, they also learn that anxiety/fear/disgust and intense urges to ritualize do not last forever and will eventually dissipate. In addition to this habituation, patients gain a sense of mastery over their OCD by learning that they can tolerate doubt, uncertainty, and the presence of unwanted thoughts. Rather than teaching patients to resist or "fix" their anxiety/fear/disgust, this type of therapy helps patients understand and accept that negative emotions are inevitable, a normal part of life that everyone experiences, and are not inherently dangerous. As patients learn to tolerate distress and complete tasks even while experiencing these distressing emotions, OCD loosens its grip and patients re-gain control over their lives.

VRET for OCD follows this same theoretical framework, but patients engage in virtual exposures, rather than or in addition to *in vivo* or imaginal exposures. Virtual exposures are specifically tailored to elicit anxiety, fear, and/or disgust by triggering the patient's obsessions. Patients are instructed to fully immerse themselves into the virtual exposure and are coached to refrain from compulsions, safety behaviors, or other strategies to reduce distress, while engaging with the virtual environment. Research investigating VRET for OCD is more limited than for anxiety disorders, but the results of existing studies are compelling and suggest that VRET may be a particularly effective treatment modality for patients with OCD. A brief review of existing research emphasizes the efficacy of virtual exposures for activating patients' obsessions, eliciting fear/anxiety/disgust reactions, triggering compulsions, reducing distress related to OCD symptoms, and increasing patients' self-efficacy.

In a series of studies testing whether virtual reality can be a helpful tool in the assessment of OCD symptoms, Kim and colleagues (2008, 2012) demonstrated that time spent checking household items (e.g., locks, stovetops, etc.) when navigating through a virtual home environment was significantly greater for participants with checking-related OCD than for participants with OCD unrelated to checking and participants without OCD. Although assessment of OCD checking symptoms was the primary focus of these studies, the results show that virtual environments can elicit checking-related obsessions and compulsions.

Belloch and colleagues (2014) examined the utility of VRET in four women who were diagnosed with OCD and reported contamination obsessions and washing compulsions as their primary symptoms. All participants had either previously completed CBT for OCD (one of whom had refused to participate in *in vivo* or imaginal exposures) or were currently in CBT for OCD.

To evaluate the virtual exposures, participants completed measures of their emotional engagement, presence, and perceptions of the reality of the virtual exposure. They also reported levels of anxiety and disgust as they completed activities within four scenarios of the Contaminated Virtual Environment (COVE). The results demonstrated that participants experienced a strong sense of presence within the virtual environment, so much so that participants experienced it as more real than artificial. The contaminated environment effectively elicited anxiety and disgust in participants and the reported levels of anxiety and disgust increased as the contamination in the virtual environment increased, indicating that virtual exposures may be effective for reducing OCD symptoms. Importantly, all participants engaged in the virtual exposures and indicated high satisfaction with the experience. This is noteworthy given the high rates of treatment refusal associated with in vivo and imaginal exposure therapy.

Laforest and colleagues (2016) evaluated whether virtual exposures could successfully elicit anxiety in people with contamination OCD. The results showed that compared to a non-clinical control group, exposure to a contaminated virtual environment elicited higher anxiety in people with OCD, as indicated by heart rate and self-report measures. Additionally, exposure to the contaminated virtual environment triggered compulsions in people with OCD. These results, particularly the convergence between self-reported distress and physiological indicators of distress, provide strong evidence that virtual exposures elicit the anxiety, fear, and/or disgust necessary for effective ERP for OCD. Similarly, in a study testing whether a virtual reality video game could trigger OCD symptoms, participants navigated a first-person perspective game that required them to walk through a house with OCD-related items like a burning gas stove, a dirty sink, and messy tables. These items were designed to trigger OCD symptoms related to contamination/cleaning, doubt/checking, and symmetry/ordering. Participants had to confront each item and then were asked if they wanted to intervene and check the item; the number of times items could be checked was unlimited. The results indicated that the game triggered higher levels of anxiety and virtual compulsions in participants with OCD as compared to those without OCD (von Bennekom et al., 2021).

Cullen and colleagues (2021) measured heart rate, respiration rate, and subjective units of distress (SUDS) as participants with OCD engaged in a virtual contamination exposure and a matched *in vivo* contamination exposure. The results indicated that both types of exposure resulted in similar levels of anxiety, as measured by self-report and physiological indicators. However, participant engagement and adherence to the exposure task was higher in the virtual exposure than in the *in vivo* exposure and the therapeutic alliance remained intact during virtual exposures. These researchers concluded that virtual reality is an effective exposure modality and may be preferrable to *in vivo* exposures due to increased patient engagement and adherence to exposure tasks.

The results of the studies discussed above show that virtual exposures can trigger a broad range of OCD obsessions and compulsions and that similar levels of anxiety/fear/disgust are provoked in virtual and *in vivo* exposures. Evidence of the effectiveness of VRET for treatment of OCD is limited to non-clinical samples, case studies, and small case series. However, the results presented below are encouraging and indicate that VRET has utility for treating OCD.

Laforest and colleagues (2016) described the treatment outcome for 3 adults with contamination OCD who completed eight sessions of ERP using virtual exposures as part of a standardized CBT treatment protocol for OCD. The results indicated that treatment resulted in a significant improvement for all three participants (though one participant's score on the Y-BOCS remained in the moderate range) and that treatment gains were maintained at a 4-month follow-up. Additionally, virtual exposures were well-tolerated by all participants, which is significant given the high rates of refusal observed for ERP in patients with OCD.

Inozu et al. (2020) investigated whether VRET could reduce contamination fear and disgust in a non-clinical sample. Participants were divided into two groups (high and low contamination fears) based on scores on the Contamination Obsessions and Washing Compulsions subscale of the Padua Inventory Washington State University Revision (PI-WSUR). While using a non-clinical sample limits the generalizability of their findings, participants included in the high contamination fears sample scored two standard deviations above the sample mean on the PI-WSUR subscales, indicating that they had significant concerns about contamination. Results demonstrated that the VRET sessions were successful in eliciting anxiety and disgust, and that the intensity of anxiety and disgust increased with the degree of dirtiness/contamination in the VR scenarios. The results also showed that VRET reduced the severity of contamination anxiety.

Further support for the utility of VRET for managing OCD is provided by a case study of a 27-year-old man in India whose harm-related OCD resulted in an inability to work and inpatient hospitalization. His OCD was characterized by obsessional images of people he knew. These images caused significant distress, which he would try to diminish by performing numerous rituals. He had previously tried ERP with imaginal exposure but could not tolerate the anxiety provoked by exposures. Virtual exposures immersed him in a 3-D environment containing repeated images of the people his obsessions centered on, combined with his voice stating the peoples 'names. Over a 2-month period, he completed 60 sessions of ERP with virtual exposures and reported that the exposures were very similar to his experience of obsessional images. This treatment led to a significant reduction in his Y-BOCS score, an 80% improvement in symptoms, and restored his ability to work without dysfunction (Dua et al., 2021).

The most promising research published on the efficacy of VRET for OCD comes from a case series presented by Miegel and colleagues (2022). The case series consisted of eight patients who were enrolled in an ongoing RCT for OCD and who had been randomized to the intervention group. These participants were diagnosed with contamination OCD and reported disgust as their primary emotion in the context of OCD. All participants had previous experience with psychotherapy and six had previously engaged in exposure therapy. VRET was completed over the course of six weeks, with four consecutive VR exposure sessions. Therapy sessions in this study were highly structured and manualized. The first two sessions prepared patients for the virtual exposures and patients were introduced to the VR equipment in a neutral VR environment during the third session. Trained therapists guided patients through the virtual exposures, which were designed to progressively increase patients 'experience of disgust while preventing engagement in compulsions and avoidance behavior. VR involved a head-mounted display and elicited contamination obsessions via increasingly filthy public bathrooms. The results of this study are encouraging. 75% of the patients responded to the first virtual exposure session with increases in SUDs rating, showing that the exposure sufficiently provoked the disgust response necessary for effective exposure therapy. There was a medium to large effect size in the reduction of OCD symptoms as measured by the Y-BOCS, including a significant decrease in obsessions. These researchers noted that it is likely that more virtual exposure sessions would result in more global improvement.

VRET Technology

Virtual reality refers to the creation of simulated environments via computer technology. In VR, users are immersed in and interact with a three-dimensional virtual environment. Virtual environments can be created using computer generated images (CGI), which yields more cartoonish images and avatars, or they can be constructed with 360° video footage, which produces highly realistic virtual environments. Headsets and other VR accessories provide sensory stimulation that enables the user to feel as though they are present in the virtual world. Users' movements and actions impact, to varying degrees, what happens in this virtual environment. Equipment required for VR can range from expensive, advanced equipment that creates highly immersive, multi-sensory virtual experiences (like HTC Vive or Meta Quest Pro) to low-cost, easily accessible equipment (like Google Cardboard) that provides immersive virtual experiences incorporating visual and auditory stimulation.

Headsets are the most recognizable VR equipment. Some headsets require cable tethers to external hardware, like PCs or gaming systems, while others are wireless and capable of transmitting information to nearby consoles or PCs. At the high end of the cost spectrum, headsets include sound sensors, eye and head motion tracking devices, and cameras; more broadly accessible, mobile headsets like Google Cardboard are shell devices designed to cover smartphone screens with lenses that create stereoscopic images, effectively converting smartphones into VR devices.

VR accessories enhance the users' experiences within the virtual environments by collecting and transmitting various types of sensory information. For example, a 3D mouse can be used to move within a virtual environment, while optical trackers monitor users 'position. Wired gloves containing various sensors can collect movement data and provide haptic feedback and tactile stimulation. Omnidirectional treadmills enable users to move in any direction while engaging with the virtual environment. Studies investigating the utility of VR for mental health purposes have added physiological sensors to VR equipment, which capture data related to heart rate, respiration rate, and skin conductance; this data can be used to supplement patients 'reports of fear and distress.

VRET for Therapy

When and Why?

When deciding which type of therapy is best for a particular patient, the patient's current socio-cultural environment must be considered. Recent trends in psychotherapy show a shift away from in-person therapy to online platforms, which may further increase the utility of VRET as it allows patients to fully participate in therapy from home. The COVID-19 global pandemic has likely escalated this movement towards online therapy platforms; data from the U.S. Census Bureau shows that the prevalence of anxiety and depression was three times higher during the first year of the pandemic compared to the year prior (Twenge & Joiner, 2020). As the pandemic continues to evolve, mental health practitioners will be faced with increasing demand for effective treatments for anxiety disorders and OCD, particularly treatments that can be fully implemented online, like VRET.

Consumer versions of VR technology are becoming increasingly affordable and accessible. Embracing this technology and using VR to create virtual exposure environments may be a more practical, ethical, and ultimately more effective means of delivering exposure therapy, especially for people with anxiety disorders and OCD. Additionally, many patients prefer VRET over other treatment options. In one study of patients with anxiety disorders, 76% of patients chose VRET over *in vivo* exposure (Garcia-Palacios et al., 2007). This preference for VRET likely applies to patients with OCD, giving another treatment option to patients who have been unwilling or unable to engage in *in vivo* or imaginal exposure therapy. Powers and Emmelkamp (2008) showed that when presented with *in vivo* and virtual exposures, patients with anxiety disorders perceived VRET as the more credible treatment option. When patients believe that an intervention is credible, they are more likely to expect it to help them, which can increase their engagement in therapy and enhance treatment response.

There is ample evidence that VRET is an effective treatment for anxiety disorders. While research on VRET for OCD is more limited, converging evidence from available studies builds a compelling case for the effectiveness of VRET for OCD. In fact, VRET may be uniquely beneficial for patients with OCD. While ERP is the evidence-based treatment for OCD, many patients do not benefit from ERP for several reasons. Studies have shown that 15-25% of patients refuse ERP, and of those who do engage, 14-25% drop out of treatment prematurely (Abramowitz, 2006; Jenike, 2004; Ong et al., 2016; Schruers et al., 2005). Of patients who engage in ERP, up to 41% do not adequately respond to the treatment (Simpson et al., 2006, 2008). This poor treatment response may reflect the difficulty of designing and carrying out *in vivo* or imaginal exposures for some obsessions and compulsions, like obsessions related to toxic chemicals or fire. Additionally, many therapists are not sufficiently trained to implement *in vivo* exposure therapy, which could also contribute to poor treatment response. VRET can remedy this by providing therapists with access to platforms containing virtual exposures that could be easily tailored to the needs of their patients.

Additional Benefits of VRET

Even for therapists who are highly skilled with implementing *in vivo* exposures as part of ERP for OCD, there are times when VRET may be a better choice. During the COVID-19 pandemic, public health measures encouraging social distancing and staying home highlighted the need for effective therapies that can be fully implemented through online platforms. Even when there is no public health emergency, patients with anxiety may be worried about meeting face-to-face due to other health conditions or seasonally high levels of illness in the community. For patients whose OCD symptoms mostly occur in their own homes, VRET allows exposures to take place in the environment within which their symptoms occur. For patients or therapists who travel frequently, VRET may be an especially attractive option because full participation in therapy is possible, regardless of location.

Virtual exposures enable patients to go places they could not practically or safely go in real life. Exposures involving flying in planes, poisonous snakes, toxic chemicals, or visiting a crowd during a pandemic are just a few examples of what is possible with VRET. Without access to virtual reality technology, imaginal exposure must be used to address fears related to these impractical or potentially risky situations. Many patients, particularly those who have anxiety, have difficulty creating detailed and emotionally engaging imaginal exposures. Virtual exposures, on the other hand, allow patients to fully immerse themselves in realistic, multisensory virtual experiences. Additionally, virtual exposures can be designed to elicit higher levels of fear than is possible with *in vivo* exposures, which can enhance treatment response and require fewer exposure sessions.

For many patients with OCD, VRET is a more cost-effective treatment approach. In traditional *in vivo* ERP, considerable time is required for planning and travel. VRET is far less time-consuming; exposure sessions can be conducted in the patient's home with no additional travel or logistical planning. It is reasonable to think that VRET may be more cost effective in that patients could complete therapy in a shorter timeframe than is possible with *in vivo* ERP. Increases in self-efficacy have been consistently observed in VRET; increased beliefs in one's ability to persevere and complete exposure tasks may facilitate a more rapid progression through the exposure hierarchy, meaning that the time spent in therapy may be reduced with VRET (Cote & Bouchard, 2005; Powers & Emmelkamp, 2008; Meyerbroker et al., 2022). Further, with VRET, patients can complete multiple exposures in one session, which may also speed up treatment gains.

VRET can be used in the patients 'homes, in the therapists 'office, or in a hybrid manner that allows patients to first experience exposures in the therapist's office and then complete homework assignments at home. This flexibility also makes VRET a good fit for patients and therapists 'who travel frequently by allowing full engagement in treatment from virtually any location. It also means that people in remote areas or living in communities where there are no trained exposure therapists can access effective treatment without traveling. Advances in technology enable full participation in VRET without purchasing costly equipment. Therapists may choose to purchase more expensive, advanced VR systems for use in office, but patients can access VR at a low cost through platforms like Google Cardboard.

There are often safety and ethical challenges inherent in conducting exposures in real-world settings. It is difficult to protect patient confidentiality when patients are completing exposures in public, especially if exposures involve interactions with other people. Additionally, some exposures are potentially risky; exposures for patients who fear they may jump off a cliff or onto the third rail of the subway can be risky. These concerns could be eliminated by using VRET, which enables patients to fully engage in ERP in the privacy and safety of their own homes.

VRET is also preferrable to many *in vivo* exposures in that the therapist has greater control over many aspects of the exposure, including the duration, intensity, and frequency of exposure sessions. This means that patients can progress through exposure sessions gradually without being exposed to situations that would be overwhelming or too difficult to handle. This builds patients 'self-efficacy due to their increased sense of control and success with moving through the exposures. For exposures that involve interacting with other people, like for patients who fear they may say or do something offensive to others, therapists can also control the reactions of others in virtual exposures.

Issues to Consider

While VRET has many advantages over *in vivo* exposure therapy, there are some things to consider during treatment planning. Until very recently, the cost of VR equipment was high, meaning that very few patients could possess the necessary equipment. However, recent trends show that consumer versions of VR technology are becoming increasingly affordable, and access is likely to significantly increase (Donker et al., 2019; Lindner et al., 2019; Widerhold & Riva, 2019). The availability of low-cost VR equipment like Google Cardboard makes this technology available to anyone who has a smartphone. These platforms transform smartphones into VR headsets using drop-in cardboard holders and make accessing virtual exposures as simple as downloading an app.

Studies investigating the utility of virtual exposures have noted that some patients have difficulty engaging emotionally with VR exposures. In a meta-analysis comparing attrition rates between traditional *in* vivo exposure therapy and VRET for anxiety disorders, Benbow and Anderson (2019) reported an attrition rate of 16% across 46 studies (total N = 1,057). The most frequently reported reason for dropping out was difficulty immersing in the virtual environment. However, Ling and colleagues (2014) noted that it is important to consider the type of VR technology being used in studies and reported that more advanced VR technology leads to higher immersion into the virtual exposure and suggested that drop-out rates would subsequently be lower for VRET using advanced technology. Virtual environments created using CGI tend to look more cartoonish and less real, which may inhibit patients 'sense of presence and fail to trigger patients ' distress. On the other hand, virtual exposure environments created with 360° video images may increase presence and immersion and the reality of these images is more likely to trigger patients 'symptoms. Therapists may also recognize that when patients report difficulty engaging with virtual exposures, this may be a signal that the patient is avoiding engagement in the exposure due to difficulty tolerating distress caused by the experience. Additional focus on distress tolerance skills and using motivational interviewing techniques to increase patient motivation for engagement in the therapeutic process may help address these difficulties.

Finally, studies have shown that some patients drop out of VRET due to a type of VR-induced motion sickness, termed "cybersickness" (Kim et al., 2018). Cybersickness can feel like motion sickness and may involve nausea, dizziness, disorientation, headaches, and eye strain. Cybersickness is triggered when your brain receives contradictory sensory information, like when your eyes perceive rapid movement while the body is not actually moving. People who are prone to cybersickness can learn techniques for managing it, like focusing on a steady object. The multi-sensory experiences created by more advanced VR technology may decrease discrepant sensory information and reduce the likelihood of cybersickness.

There have also been concerns regarding whether VRET is safe for patients who experience photosensitive seizures (Tychsen & Thio, 2020). More research is necessary to clarify whether optimization of VR technology will result in greater tolerance of VR and to standardize safety protocols for patients with medical conditions. However, it is worth noting that the studies described in this treatment guide have reported either similar or lower drop-out rates compared to traditional in vivo exposure therapy, suggesting that the proportion of patients who experience negative effects from VR exposures is low.

Conclusion

OCD can be debilitating, and sufferers can struggle with shame. The more that therapists and individuals in the public become educated about OCD, the more quickly we can break the stigma and reduce the shame. The good news is that even though we don't know exactly what causes OCD, there are effective therapies to address it. If a patient suspects that they may have OCD, it is important to identify a treatment provider who is specifically trained in its treatment. Therapists expect that potential patients will ask questions about that therapist's knowledge and experience with specific maladies. Don't be afraid to ask what training the therapist has in treating OCD, how long have they been treating OCD, how many patients have they worked with who have had OCD and what is their treatment approach? Once a patient identifies a qualified clinician, progress can often be achieved more quickly than one might expect. Don't be afraid to reach out for help because the sooner you get help the more successful you will be in taking charge of OCD before it takes charge of you.

About the Author

Andrew E. Colsky, JD, LLM, LPC, LMHC is an author and clinician specializing in the treatment of Obsessive Compulsive Disorder, Anxiety and Tourette Syndrome. He is a serial entrepreneur who is passionate about improving mental healthcare and is always striving to do what others believe can't be done. He created Doubt Reduction and Inhibitory Learning (DRIL) therapy, drawing from both Exposure and Response Prevention (ERP) therapy and Inference-Based Cognitive Behavioral Therapy (ICBT). Born from his desire to bring innovation to the mental health field, he founded Prescription XRT (www.rxxrt.com), a first-of-its-kind exposure therapy platform providing therapists the ability to conduct life-like exposures with their clients virtually anywhere. He is a member of the International OCD Foundation, Anxiety and Depression Association of America, Association of Behavioral and Cognitive Therapies and Tourette Association of America.

References

Abramowitz, J. S. (2006). The psychological treatment of obsessive-compulsive disorder. *Canadian Journal of Psychiatry, 51*(7), 407-416. https://doi.org/10.1383/psyt.3.6.68.38210

American Psychiatric Association. (2013). *Diagnostic and statistical manual of mental disorders* (5th ed.). https://doi.org/10.1176/appi.books.9780890425596

Anderson, P. L., Zimand, E., Hodges, L. F., & Rothbaurn, B. O. (2005). Cognitive behavioral therapy for public-speaking anxiety using virtual reality for exposure. *Depression and Anxiety, 22*(3), 156-158.
https://doi.org/10.1002/da.20090

Belloch, A., Cabedo, E., Carrio, C., Lozano-Quilis, J. A., Gil-Gomez, J. A., & Gil-Gomez, H. (2014). Virtual reality exposure for OCD: Is it feasible? *Revista de Psicopatologia y Psicologia Clinica, 19*(1), 37.
https://doi.org/10.5944/rppc.vol.19.num.1.2014.12981

Benbow, A. A., & Anderson, P. L. (2019). A meta-analytic examination of attrition in virtual reality exposure therapy for anxiety disorders. *Journal of Anxiety Disorders, 61,* 18-26. https://doi.org/10.1016/j.janxdis.2018.06.006

Carl, E., Stein, A. T., Levihn-Coon, A., Pogue, J. R., Rothbaum, B., Emmelkamp, P., Asmundson, G. J. G., Carlbring, P., & Powers, M. B. (2019). Virtual reality exposure therapy for anxiety and related disorders: A meta-analysis of randomized controlled trials. *Journal of Anxiety Disorders, 61,* 27-36. https://doi.org/10.1016/j.janxdis.2018.08.003

Cote, S., & Bouchard, S. (2005). Cognitive mechanisms underlying virtual reality exposure. *Cyberpsychology and Behavior, 12,* 121-129.

Cote, S. & Bouchard, S. (2009). Cognitive mechanisms underlying virtual reality exposure. *CyberPsychology & Behavior, 12*(2), 121-129. https://doi.org/10.1089/cpb.2008.0008

Craske, M. G., Treanor, M., Conway, C. C., Zbozinek, T., & Vervliet, B. (2014). Maximizing exposure therapy: An inhibitory learning approach. *Behaviour Research and Therapy, 58,* 10-23. https://doi.org/10.1016/j.brat.2014.04.006

Cullen, A. J., Dowling, N. L., Segrave, R., Carter, A., Yucel, M. (2021). Exposure therapy in a virtual environment: Validation in obsessive compulsive disorder. *Journal of Anxiety Disorders, 80,* 102404. https://doi.org/10.1016/j.janxdis.2021.102404

Deacon, B. J., & Abromowitz, J. S. (2004). Cognitive and behavioral treatments for anxiety disorders: A review of meta-analytic findings. *Journal of Clinical Psychology, 60*(4), 429-441. https://doi.org/10.1002/jclp.10255

Donker, T., Cornelisz, I., van Klaveren, C., van Straten, A., Carlbring, P., Cuijpers, P., & van Gelder, J.-L. (2019). Effectiveness of self-guided app-based virtual reality cognitive behavior therapy for acrophobia: A randomized clinical trial. *JAMA Psychiatry, 76*(7), 682-690. https://doi.org/10.1001/jamapsychiatry.2019.0219

Dua, D., Jagota, G., & Grover, S. (2021). Management of obsessive-compulsive disorder with virtual reality-based exposure. *Industrial Psychiatry Journal, 30,* 179-181. https://doi.org/10.4103/ipj.ipj_33_19

Fernandez, T. V., Leckman, J. F., & Pitterger, C. (2018). Genetic susceptibility in obsessive-compulsive disorder. *Handbook of Clinical Neurology, 148,* 767-781.

Foa, E. B., Yadin, E., & Lichner, T. K. (2012). *Exposure and response (ritual) prevention for obsessive-compulsive disorder: Therapist guide (treatments that work).* Oxford University Press.

Garcia-Palacios, A., Botella, C., Hoffman, H., & Fabregat, S. (2007). Comparing acceptance and refusal rates of virtual reality exposure vs. *in vivo* exposure by patients with specific phobias. *CyberPsychology & Behavior, 10,* 722-724. https://doi.org/10.1089/cpb.2007.9962

Grayson, J. (2003). *Freedom from obsessive-compulsive disorder: a personalized recovery program for living with uncertainty.* Penguin-Putnam.

Goodman, W.K., Storch, E. A., & Sheth, S. A. (2021). Harmonizing the neurobiology and treatment of obsessive-compulsive disorder. *American Journal of Psychiatry, 178*(1), 17-29. https://doi.org/10.1176/appi.ajp.2020.20111601
Inozu, M., Celikcan, U., Akin, B., & Cicek, N. M. (2020). The use of virtual reality (VR) exposure for reducing contamination fear and disgust: Can VR be an effective alternative exposure technique to *in vivo? Journal of Obsessive-Compulsive and Related Disorders, 25,* https://doi.org/10.1016/j.jocrd.2020.100518

Jenicke, M. A. (2004). Obsessive-compulsive disorder. *The New England Journal of Medicine, 350*(3), 256-263. https://doi.org/10.1016/B978-0-12-385157-4.01073-3

Julien, D., O'Connor, K., & Aardema, F. (2016). The inference-based approach to obsessive-compulsive disorder: a comprehensive review of its etiological model, treatment efficacy, and model of change. *Journal of Affective Disorders, 202,* 187-196. https://doi.org/10.1016/j.jad.2016.05.060

Kim, C. H., Cha, K. R., Kim, S. I., Kim, K. W., & Jon, D. I. (2008). Virtual reality assessment of checking symptoms in patients with obsessive compulsive disorder. *Journal of Affective Disorders, 107,* S121. https://doi.org/10.1016/j.jad.2007.12.142

Kim, K., Roh, D., Kim, C. H., Cha, K. R., Rosenthal, M. Z., & Kim, S. I. (2012). Comparison of checking behavior in adults with or without checking symptoms of obsessive-compulsive disorder using a novel computer-based measure. *Computer Methods and Programs in Biomedicine, 108*(1), 434-441. https://doi.org/10.1016/j.cmpb.2012.03.014

Kim, H., Shin, J. E., Hong, Y.-J., Shin, Y.-B., Shin, Y. S., Han, K., Kim, J. J., & Choi, S.-H. (2018). Aversive eye gaze during a speech in virtual environment in patients with social anxiety disorder. *Australian & New Zealand Journal of Psychiatry, 52*(3), 279-285. https://doi.org/10.1177/0004867417714335

Laforest, M., Bouchard, S., Bosse, J., & Mesly, O. (2016). Effectiveness of *in virtuo* exposure and response prevention treatment using cognitive-behavioral therapy for obsessive-compulsive disorder: A study based on a single-case study protocol. *Frontiers in Psychiatry, 7,* 99. https://doi.org/10.3389/fpsyt.2016.00099

Laforest, M., Bouchard, S., Cretu, A., & Mesly, O. (2016). Inducing an anxiety response using a contaminated virtual environment: validation of a therapeutic tool for obsessive-compulsive disorder. *Frontiers in ICT, 3, Article 18.* https://doi.10.3389/fict.2016.00018

Lindner, P., Miloff, A., Zetterlund, E., Reuterskiold, L., Andersson, G. & Carlbring, P. (2019). Attitudes toward and familiarity with virtual reality therapy among practicing cognitive behavioral therapists: A cross-sectional survey study in an era of consumer VR platforms. *Frontiers in Psychology, 10,* 176. https://doi.org/10.3389/fpsyg.2019.00176

Ling, Y., Nefs, H. T., Morina, N., Heynderickx, I., & Brinkman, W. (2014). A meta-analysis on the relationship between self-reported presence and anxiety in virtual reality exposure therapy for anxiety disorders. *Plos One, 9*(5), e96144.https://dx.doi.org/10.1371/journal.pone.0096144

Ludvik, D., Bosche, M. J., & Neumann, D. L. (2015). Effective behavioural strategies for reducing disgust in contamination-related OCD: A review. *Clinical Psychology Review, 42,* 116-129. https://doi.org/10.1016/j.cpr.2015.07.001

Mahjani, B., Klei, L., Hultman, C. M., Larsson, H., Devlin, B., Buxbaum, J. D., Sandin, S., & Grice, D. E. (2020). Maternal effects as causes of risk for obsessive-compulsive disorder. *Biological Pyschiatry, 87,* 1045-1051. https://doi.org/10.1016/j.biopsych.2020.01.006

Mataix-Cols, D., Boman, M., Monzani, B., Ruck, C., Serlachius, E., Langstrom, N, & Lichenstein, P. (2013). Population-based multigenerational family clustering study of obsessive-compulsive disorder. *JAMA Psychiatry, 70,* 709-717. https://doi.org/10.1001/jamapsychiatry.2013.3

McMahon, E. & Boelt, D. (2022). *Virtual reality therapy for anxiety: A guide for therapists.* Routledge. https://doi.org/10.4324/9781003154068

Meyerbroker, K., & Emmelkamp, P. M. G. (2010). Virtual reality exposure therapy in anxiety disorders: a systematic review of process-and-outcome studies. *Depression and Anxiety, 27,* 933-944.http://doi.org/10.1002/da.20734

Meyerbroker, K., Morina, N., Kerkhof, G. A., & Emmelkamp, P. M. G. (2022) Potential predictors of virtual reality exposure therapy for fear of flying: anxiety sensitivity, self-efficacy and the therapeutic alliance. *Cognitive Therapy and Research, 46,* 646-654.
https://doi.org/10.1007/s10608-021-10269-7

Miegel, F., Bucker, L., Kuhn, S., Mostajeran, F., Moritz, S., Baumeister, A., Lohse, L., Blomer, J., Grzella, K., & Jelinek, L. (2022). Exposure and response prevention in virtual reality for patients with contamination-related obsessive-compulsive disorder: a case series. *Psychiatric Quarterly, 93,* 861-882. https://doi.org/10.1007/s11126-022-09992-5

Morina, N., Brinkman, W-P., Hartanto, D., Kampmann, I. L., & Emmelkamp, P. M. G. (2015). Social interactions in virtual reality exposure therapy: A proof-of-concept pilot study. *Technology and Health Care, 23,* 581-589. https://doi.org/10.3233/THC-151014

O'Connor, K., and Aardema, F. (2012) Clinician's Handbook for Obsessive-Compulsive Disorder. John Wiley and Sons Ltd. https://doi.org/10.1002/9781119960027

Ong, C. W., Clyde, J. W., Bluett, E. J., Levin, M. E., & Twohig, M. P. (2016). Dropout rates in exposure with response prevention

for obsessive-compulsive disorder: What to the data really say? *Journal of Anxiety Disorders, 40,* 8-17.
https://doi.org/10.1016/j.anxdis.2016.03.006

Opris, D., Pintea, S., Garcia-Palacios, A., Botella, C., Szamoskozi, S., & David, D. (2012). Virtual reality exposure therapy in anxiety disorders: a quantitative meta-analysis. *Depression and Anxiety, 29,* 85-93. https://doi.org/10.1007/s10608-021-10269-7

Piacentini, J. Bergman, R. L., Chang, S., Langley, A., Peris, T. S., Wood, J. J., & McCracken, J. (2011). Controlled comparison of family cognitive behavioral therapy and psychoeducation/relaxation training for child obsessive-compulsive disorder. *Journal of the American Academy of Child and Adolescent Psychiatry, 50*(11), 1149-1161.
https://doi.or/10.1016/j.jaac.2011.08.003
Powers, M. B., & Emmelkamp, P. M. G. (2008). Virtual reality exposure therapy for anxiety disorders: A meta-analysis. *Journal of Anxiety Disorders, 22,* 561-569.
https://doi.org/10.1016/j.janxdis.2007.04.006

Quero, S., Perez-Ara, M. A., Breton-Lopez, J., Garcia-Palacios, A., Banos, R. M., & Botella, C. (2014). Acceptability of virtual reality interoceptive exposure for the treatment of panic disorder with agoraphobia. *British Journal of Guidance and Counselling, 42*(2), 123-137. https://doi.org/10.1080/03069885.2013.852159

Reeves, R., Curran, D., Gleeson, A., & Hanna, D. (2022). A meta-analysis of the efficacy of virtual reality and in vivo exposure therapy as psychological interventions for public speaking anxiety. *Behavior Modification, 46*(4), 937-965.
https://doi.org/10.1177/0145445521991102

Simpson, H. B., Huppert, J. D., Petkova, E., Foa, E. B., & Liebowitz, M. R. (2006). Response versus remission in obsessive-compulsive disorder. *Journal of Clinical Psychiatry, 67*(2), 269-276. https://doi.org/10.4088/JCP.v67n0214

Simpson, H. B., Foa, E. B., Liebowitz, M. R., Ledley, D. R., Huppert, J. D., Cahill, S., Vermes, D., Schmidt, A. B., Hembree, E., Franklin, M., Campeas, R., Hahn, C.-G., & Petkova, E. (2008). A randomized, controlled trial of cognitive-behavioral therapy for augmenting pharmacotherapy in obsessive-compulsive disorder. *The American Journal of Psychiatry, 165*(5), 621-630. https://doi.org/10.1176/appi.ajp.2007.07091440

Schruers, K., Koning, K., Luermans, J., Haack, M. J., & Griez, E. (2005). Obsessive-compulsive disorder: A critical review of therapeutic perspectives. *Acta Psychiatrica Scandinavica, 111*(4), 261-271. https://doi.org/10.1111/j.1600-0447.2004.0052.x

Twenge, J. M., & Joiner, T. E. (2020). U.S. Census Bureau-assessed prevalence of anxiety and depressive symptoms in 2019 and during the 2020 COVID-19 pandemic. *Depression & Anxiety, 37,* 954-956. https://doi.org/10.1002/da.23077

Tychsen, L., & Thio, L. L. (2020). Concern of photosensitive seizures evoked by 3D video displays or virtual reality headsets in children: Current perspective. *Eye and Brain, 12,* 45-48. https://doi.org/10.2147/EB.S233195

Van Bennekom, M. J., de Koning, P. P., Gevonden, M. J., Kasanmoentalib, M. S., & Denys, D. (2021). A virtual reality game to assess OCD symptoms. *Frontiers in Psychiatry, 11,* 550165. https://doi.org/10/3389/fpsyt.2020.550165

Wallach, H. S., Safir, M. P., & Bar-Zvi, M. (2009). Virtual reality cognitive behavior therapy for public speaking anxiety: a randomized clinical trial. *Behavior Modification, 33,* 314-338. https://doi.org/10.1177/0145445509331926

Wechsler, T. F., Kumpers, F., & Muhlberger, A. (2019). Inferiority or even superiority of virtual reality exposure therapy in phobias? – A systematic review and quantitative meta-analysis on randomized controlled trials specifically comparing the efficacy of virtual reality exposure to gold standard in vivo exposure in agoraphobia, specific phobia, and social phobia. *Frontiers in Psychology, 10.* https://doi.org/10.3389/fpsyg.2019.01758

Wiederhold, B. K., & Riva, G. (2019). Virtual reality therapy: Emerging topics and future challenges. *Cyberpsychology, Behavior, and Social Networking, 22*(1), 3-6. https://doi.org/10.1089/cyber.2018.29136.bkw

Wu, M. S., McGuire, J. F., Martino, C., Phares, V., Selles, R. R., & Storch, E. A. (2016). A meta-analysis of family accommodation and OCD symptom severity. *Clinical Psychology Review, 45,* 34-44. https://doi.org/10.1016/j.cpr.2016.03.003

Appendix

Treatment Motivator Forms

OCD as relates to self:

Statements	Explain	Rating of staying in this position	Rating if you were relieved of this situation
Consider how much time in a day is devoted to OCD obsessions and compulsions.			
Consider the level of distress you feel when dealing with OCD.			
Consider the things you have missed out on or avoided because of OCD.			
Consider how you have felt around others due to your OCD.			
Consider how you feel about having OCD.			
Consider employment-related issues due to OCD.			
Consider financial issues related to OCD.			

OCD as relates to others:

Statements	Explain	Rating of staying in this position	Rating if you were relieved of this situation
Consider whether you have asked others to accommodate your OCD.			
Consider OCD's impact on other's ability to spend time with you and share in your life.			
Consider how your reaction to OCD may have impacted others.			
Consider whether your OCD has impacted others by making them late to, or miss events all together.			
Consider what monetary impact your OCD may have had on others.			

Self-Monitoring Form

OCD SELF-MONITORING FORM: Date: _______________________

Time	Situation/ Thought	SUDS (0-100)	Describe Ritual	Minutes Spent
12:00 - 1:00 AM				
1:00 - 2:00 AM				
2:00 - 3:00 AM				
3:00 - 4:00 AM				
4:00 - 5:00 AM				
5:00 - 6:00 AM				
6:00 - 7:00 AM				
7:00 - 8:00 AM				
8:00 - 9:00 AM				
9:00 - 10:00 AM				
10:00 - 11:00 AM				
11:00 - 12:00 PM				
12:00 - 1:00 PM				
1:00 - 2:00 PM				
2:00 - 3:00 PM				
3:00 - 4:00 PM				
4:00 - 5:00 PM				
5:00 - 6:00 PM				
6:00 - 7:00 PM				
7:00 - 8:00 PM				
8:00 - 9:00 PM				
9:00 - 10:00 PM				
10:00 - 11:00 PM				
11:00 - 12:00 AM				

Obsessive Doubt Tracking Form

Obsessive Doubt Tracking

1) Things beyond your control, 2) Emotion over logic, 3) Confirmation bias, 4) Complex over simple thinking,
5) Possibility becomes probability, 6) Overgeneralization, 7) Anecdotes, 8) Hearsay, 9) False causation

What is the Obsessive Thought?	Facts/ Senses Proof (See, smell, touch, taste, hear)	Who are you according to your core values?	What is the Obsessive Doubt	Obsessive doubts proof to support it
My hands may be contaminated and I could spread it and that could make me sick.	I went to the store and bought groceries. I do not see any dirt on my hands, I do not feel anything sticky, I do not smell anything on my hands.	I value being a clean person with good personal hygiene.	I have no evidence of any dirt on my hands but I just can't believe it. I went out and touched things so I must be contaminated.	2, 5

Exposure Hierarchy Form

SUDS											
Exposure											

Resources

Prescription XRT. An online exposure resource for sharing real 360 degree photos and videos with the ability to generate any desired image as needed using Artificial Intelligence technology. This resource can be used in-person or remotely for Telehealth. (www.rxxrt.com)

Inference-Based Cognitive Behavioral Therapy official website. (www.icbt.online)

International OCD Foundation. Provides information, resources, a directory of practitioners and a list of support groups. (www.iocdf.org)

Anxiety and Depression Association of America. Provides information and a directory of practitioners. (www.adaa.org)

List of therapists using virtual reality in therapy. (www.vrtherapistsinternational.com)

Society for Virtual Reality Therapy. (www.svrt.org)

American Medical Extended Reality Association (www.amxra.org)

www.ingramcontent.com/pod-product-compliance
Lightning Source LLC
Chambersburg PA
CBHW051056250726
48656CB00001B/330